Henry Stacy Marks

Pen And Pencil Sketches Marks 1

Vol. I.

Henry Stacy Marks

Pen And Pencil Sketches Marks 1
Vol. I.

ISBN/EAN: 9783337009540

Printed in Europe, USA, Canada, Australia, Japan

Cover: Foto ©Thomas Meinert / pixelio.de

More available books at **www.hansebooks.com**

Henry Stacy Marks, R.A.
From the Portrait by W.W. Ouless, R.A.

PEN AND PENCIL SKETCHES ❋❋❋ By

HENRY STACY MARKS

R.A. ❋❋❋

IN TWO VOLUMES

VOL. I

London

CHATTO & WINDUS, PICCADILLY

1894

TO

MARY

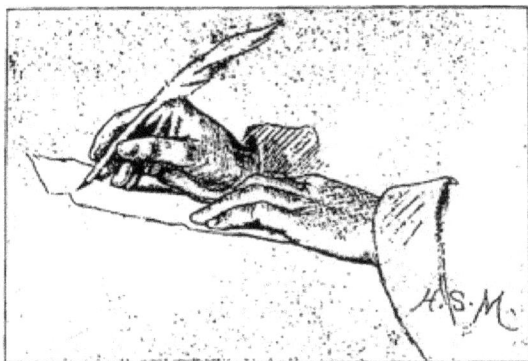

PREFACE

WHATEVER else may be said of this work,
I can confidently declare that it was neither
written with the remotest idea of supplying a want
long felt, nor undertaken at the solicitation of en-
thusiastic friends. I confess to being as sceptical of
the existence of such long-felt wants, as I am with
regard to the statements which we so frequently read,
when a man eminent in the political world, or a
celebrity in the Church, the Law, or a great General
or Naval Commander is removed from the scene, that
his loss is irreparable. Inexorable time shows in a

few short months that the loss is not so irreparable as was at first supposed. The gap is filled up by some one else, the world continues to revolve, and goes on much the same as before. So with the entreaties and suggestions of friends to publish perhaps a volume of verse. I have my doubts, and sometimes fancy they are having a joke at the would-be author's expense, or that their suggestions exist only in his imagination.

In place of writing disquisitions and views of art, except in a humble way, I have ventured to give a few of my impressions of London, its omnibuses, theatres, and music-halls, &c., its noises and other delights. Some words on the dog, the friend of man, whose praises have been sounded by hundreds of trumpets, may serve to show his admirers that there are still other points of view from which his claims to universal perfection may be regarded and enforced. In what I have said about personal friends, I have endeavoured, as far as possible, to give anecdotes that have not appeared in print before, as in the case of Fred Walker and others. The anecdotes of Mr. Ruskin and selection from his letters will be found interesting, as showing in some degree another view of his many-sided nature. In writing of my

friends, whether those of youth or manhood, it will be
found, I hope, that I have said nothing cynical or ill-
natured. The turn for sarcasm, which it was said
I had in my salad days, was, I am inclined to think,
rather a habit of seeing everything on its ludicrous
side, than the outcome of a malevolent disposition.
It was "meat and drink to me to see a clown," and I
seldom resisted the temptation to chaff an individual
who answered to that description ; but still I treated
him as Walton did the worm with which he baited his
hook, "as if I loved him." As years advance, the
milk of human kindness flows in a gentler stream—
one looks less for peculiarities than for good qualities
in man, and while not expecting too much of human
nature, one is glad to find more than enough to esteem
and love. Pleasant as the occupation of writing the
following pages has been, that pleasure has been often
tinctured with sadness, as the thought would occur of
the friends that are gone—of the old familiar faces
that shall be seen no more. With the memory of
each one is associated a flood of recollections, whether
friend or comrade cut down in the flower of youth
with hopes and aspirations unrealised, or departed
full of years, the long day's work accomplished.

Among the few qualifications of which I can boast

is that of a good memory; this has stood me in good
stead in the present work, for such diaries as I have
kept are the reverse of voluminous, recording little
but the work of each day—some place visited, or
other matter of private interest. Writing one's Recollections trains and improves the memory greatly.
When thinking over what would be suitable for
these pages, either in odd moments of the day or in
the silent watches of those nights when the inestim-
able boon of sleep is denied, and hour after hour is
tolled from neighbouring steeples with ghastly irrita-
tion (a terrible time),—it is, I say, at such moments
that I have been surprised to find how a face, a
rhyme, a scene, or incident, that had long been forgotten, has been recalled with an accuracy as
strange as it was vivid. This may not be a novel
experience to others, nor do I offer it as a profound
or original observation.

George D. Leslie, whose "Letters to Marco" I
hope all my readers have read, and admired for
their love of nature and the simple unaffected style in
which they are written, is the only friend to whom
I have read passages from this book. Though not
one of my oldest friends, we were very intimately
connected at one time, when we occupied the upper

part of a house which stood, and still stands, at a corner in Elgin Road, leading into Maida Vale. There was no regular studio, no " top light," and painters' glass-houses were comparatively a rarity ; but each painting-room, Leslie's on the first, mine on the second floor, had no fewer than five windows: a circumstance that Leslie, who was then beginning to paint open-air pictures, utilised in getting novel effects of lighting. His " Rose Harvest," which he fancied contributed in a measure to his ultimate election as A.R.A., was painted here. He gave me some hints for my book, and some anecdotes of which I availed myself in the text.

I have to express my grateful acknowledgments to my friends, the Editors of the " Spectator," for granting me permission to make use of some of my contributions to that journal. A lifetime had elapsed since last we met : the interview was short, but very pleasant. They were the same as ever, kind-hearted and friendly—though Time had furrowed our faces more deeply, and greyed the heads that had been black or brown.

And I must refer gratefully to the kindness shown me by my friend Byron Webber, who has been my literary adviser throughout, ever ready with valuable counsel and cheering words when I was in despondent moods. For all which offices I tender him my best thanks.

And now, go forth, my book. May my friends be lenient with you, and my critics merciful.

H. S. M.

17 HAMILTON TERRACE, N.W.
September 1894.

CHARLES KEENE.
By Hubert Herkomer, 1870.

CHARLES KEENE.
By Hubert Herkomer, 1870.

CONTENTS

CHAPTER I

CHILDHOOD

CHAPTER II

"*LEIGH'S,*" 1845-1851

CHAPTER III

PARIS, 1852—*BELGIUM,* 1860

CHAPTER IV

AFTER PARIS—CLAYTON AND BELL—DUBLIN,
1853-1859

CHAPTER V

FREDERICK WALKER

CHAPTER VI

FREDERICK WALKER AND RUSKIN

CHAPTER VII

CHARLES KEENE

CHAPTER VIII

"PUNCH:" ITS ARTS AND ARTISTS

CHAPTER XI

ARTHUR J. LEWIS—JUNIOR ETCHING CLUB—
MORAY MINSTRELS

CHAPTER XII

DECORATION, 1859

CHAPTER XIII

ROYAL ACADEMY—OLD WATER-COLOUR

LIST OF ILLUSTRATIONS

IN VOL. I

PEN AND PENCIL SKETCHES

CHAPTER I

CHILDHOOD

I HAVE heard, on the best possible authority, that I was born at a house in Great Portland Street (the number of which I forget), on the morning of the 13th September 1829. I was the fourth child and the third son, two having died before I was born. I was baptized at All Saints' Church, Langham Place. As an infant, I was remarkably plump and of such Michael-Angelesque proportions, that my sister, my senior by two years, would proclaim to all

she met, " I've dot *suss* a buzzer!" and " Suss"
became my nickname for many years.   Of my
infancy I remember nothing.   My father had been
bred to the law, and practised for some years as a
solicitor in Great Russell Street, Bloomsbury.   Being
the eldest son, he had, on the death of my grand-
father, to relinquish the law and continue the business of coachbuilder, in premises with a considerable
frontage in Langham Place, that extended as far back
as Great Portland Street, and were known as Marks
& Co.'s.   They have been rebuilt and rebuilt since.
The Langham Bazaar, St. George's Hall, and the
Queen's Hall, just completed, in turn have occupied
the site.   My earliest recollections are of the dwell-
ing-house connected with the business premises.
This overlooked a spacious yard leading out of
Great Portland Street, and consisted of two storeys
built above the ground, the space beneath being
occupied by storerooms and standing-places for
carriages.   In the yard were sheds for cleaning
and washing the latter.   At the end farthest from
the house was a staircase, and a movable platform
and crane for conveying vehicles to the floor above,
which consisted of long lofts or galleries for the
housing and sale of carriages of all kinds, from the
old-fashioned landau to the more modern stanhope
or cabriolet.   The upper lofts at the back of the
house were occupied by various shops—the body-

makers, harness-makers, trimmers, and so on. The yard sheds were partly occupied by such carriages as were let on hire for the day ; and well do I remember on a Derby or Ascot morning the post-boys arriving with their horses from Newman's (now gone for ever). How smart and clean they looked in their blue jackets, white hats and breeches, shining top-boots, and flowers in their button-holes, as they trotted gaily forth in the morning—how dusty and travel-stained on their return in the evening ! Most of the boys had apparently re-freshed themselves pretty freely on the way back, but I never knew one who refused the glass of gin which was offered him as he got off his saddle. My father used to provide a goodly store of bottles of that beverage on these occasions, and I never heard him complain that any of the liquor had been left. When old enough, I was sent to a school in Foley Place, now Langham Street, conducted by a Mr. and Mrs. Paul. Many, many years after, when calling on my friend Eyre Crowe, I found him painting in a room which I recognised as the one in which I had shed many bitter tears and endured much mental agony as a school-boy. I have heard many say that the happiest time in their lives was that which they passed at school. I cannot agree with them, and can see no reason why I should ever be likely to alter that opinion.

As far back as I can remember, my father and mother were strict Dissenters. They had been Church of England people, and great theatre-goers in the earlier days of their marriage. I discovered this latter fact by peeping into a cupboard, the door of which had been left unlocked, and seeing rolls of flimsy, coarsely printed paper, which after experience told me were playbills.

One of my brothers, two sisters, and I were taken of a Sunday morning to Craven Chapel in some court leading out of Regent Street. The chapel still exists, though it seems much smaller than when I used to hear sermons there. The minister was Dr. Leifchild, a goodly, portly man with a sonorous voice and good staying powers. His discourses appeared to the childish mind of inordinate length, and perhaps a little ponderous in matter. We children used to be examined by our parents on the sermon in the afternoon, and expected to remember at least the " heads " of it ; but as the Doctor would sometimes go so far as "tenthly and lastly," it was not often we could repeat them with anything like accuracy. The closeness of the atmosphere in the chapel, combined with the eloquent denunciations of the preacher, would often send me to sleep, or cause bleeding at the nose, which enlarged the pattern on my coloured frock. Then would my father lead me home, calling on the family doctor by the way, who

administered doses or powders after the manner of
his tribe, much to my disgust and annoyance. Why
do parents persist in taking young children to these
services?—services which they are unable to understand, and which therefore are not likely to induce
reverence for sacred things in their infant minds.
The familiarity with which some ministers will treat
divine names and subjects is, to put it mildly, very
objectionable. I was walking with my mother one
day when we met one of these—an acquaintance of
hers—who, after the usual salutation, thought he
must take some notice of me, and said in a loud hard
voice, and with a smile that I did not like, " Well,
my little friend, and are you a follower of Jesus
Christ?" I would have liked to kick him, but not
knowing what to say, burst into tears, which seemed
to surprise the reverend one. I went to church for
the first time when staying at some suburb with a
coachman and his wife. Why I stayed with them I
don't know—there may have been illness at home,
or an impending increase of the population. On
the evening of the Sunday I was taken by this
worthy couple to the village church, where I was
greatly impressed and interested. The service,
simple as it was, I preferred to that of Craven
Chapel. The picturesqueness of the interior—the
evening sunlight tinted by the stained glass windows
stealing along the white-washed walls—the playing

of the organ above all, aroused whatever sentiment was in my nature. I began imagining the end of all created things, more particularly of the birds, and try as I would, I could not contain myself, and began to cry audibly. The good woman led me out, and on the way to her home endeavoured to console me by the assurance that the sparrows in the road and all other birds and beasts were but "images" and without sense. I did not believe her, but dried my eyes, and, childlike, soon forgot all about the subject.

My father was a good all-round man, fairly well read; he had a distinct literary bias, was a sound Shakespearian, and had great veneration for Dr. Johnson. He would sometimes read to us of an evening, when we would sit open-mouthed as we listened to the trial-scene in the "Merchant of Venice" or the murder in "Macbeth." "Pick-wick" was then appearing in its green covers; I don't remember ever hearing any passages from that wonderful work, but do most distinctly recollect that scene at Dotheboys Hall, and the intense excitement we felt when Nicholas Nickleby shouts "Stop!" to Squeers as he caned poor Smike, and afterwards gives the brutal, ignorant school-master a most satisfactory flogging! Though no linguist, my father knew his own tongue well, and enjoined accuracy and distinctness on his children when speaking it. He had some knowledge of music and played the violoncello. On many an evening after business hours, he and uncle and a friend of theirs—he with his cello, they with violins —would play Corelli's sonatas in the long loft, which seemed longer and gloomily mysterious illumined only by the lamps or candles of their music stands. I remember perfectly some of the airs— notably, " The Tombstone Jig! " Where is Corelli now? Is he considered old-fashioned and out of date? I have seldom heard his works performed since those early days. Fond of all games, from chess and billiards to backgammon, he was also a bit of a sportsman and a good shot. For many years in the beginning of September he used to stay for a week or fortnight with a friend who owned a farm at Bassingbourne in Cambridge-shire. I accompanied him on one or two of these expeditions. The first time was in 1837, as is shown by a book of early drawings my mother preserved, in which there are some of my sketches made at Bassingbourne, and that date written within the cover. A fact of no importance whatever, but I like, when possible, to be correct. We used to drive down, starting early from Langham Place in a two-wheeled chaise drawn by a pony, a great favourite of my father's, named "Bess." Our luggage was in the "well" of the chaise, the gun-case strapped on

behind. I enjoyed this long drive; the weather was
brilliant and the "autumn sky was blue above." We
sang blithely on the way, I the "childish treble,"
my father the deep bass, to the accompaniment of
the pony's measured trot. At some half-way inn
we stayed awhile for rest and refreshment for man,
boy, and beast, getting to the end of our journey
before nightfall. I can see my father and his
friend now, trudging through the long stubble
(no reaping-machines then), clad in corduroy knee-
breeches, gaiters, and heavy boots, their powder-
horns and shot-pouches slung over their shoulders,
accompanied by two dogs, a pointer and a setter,
just like the sportsmen we see in Bewick's tail-
pieces. And they were sportsmen too, as they
trudged along the heavy ground and through the
stubble for miles, and would think themselves well
rewarded at the end of their day with a few brace
of birds. They certainly worked harder for the
game than the sportsmen of these days of beaters
and drivers. Meanwhile, I followed them on the
pony with a young farm-labourer as guardian and
henchman. On days when the shooting was over
early, we sat under a hedge, my father with his
gun ready to let fly at the wood-pigeons which
would congregate on the roofs of the farm-buildings,
while I read aloud from the "Arabian Nights,"
which my father had caused to be packed with our

luggage—that enchanting book, which I now knew for the first time. At other times we would fly a large kite, made by my father and his host for me out of sheets of the *Times* newspaper. One afternoon when flying this, a flock of turkeys came into the field, and got their legs entangled in a quantity of the string, which had been allowed to lie on the grass. The violent tugs that my father gave to the string in trying to disentangle it from the birds, filled me with wonder and astonishment that birds' legs should be so strong as to go through such an ordeal unbroken. Another afternoon, I saw the last harvest load carried amid the shouts of the men and the shrill cries of the women ; and peeping into the kitchen one evening on my way to bed, I saw the farm-labourers enjoying their harvest-supper, or " horkey," as it was called in those regions.

My father's holiday came to an end, as all holidays will, but why will the end always come so soon ? We returned to the house at Langham Place. My father had to get into harness again, and I to go to school. Changes unknown to me were about to take place, and my father did not seem so cheerful on our return. Before leaving the old home, let me record an incident or two connected with it. Here I heard the bells tolling for the death of William IV. I remember my mother reading to

me from the *Times* the account of the fire at the
Royal Exchange—how the building, by an odd
coincidence, was destroyed while the chimes rang

A STUDY.

out the air "There's nae luck aboot the house."
I remember all the family assembled at a window
of the loft or gallery overlooking Langham Place,

A STUDY.

and seeing the Life Guards returning to their
barracks in Albany Street after the coronation of
the Queen at Westminster, and later in the day,
leaning out of the same window, I sang "God save
the Queen" at the top of my voice, much to the
amusement of the crowd beginning to assemble for
the illuminations.

A few years later the old premises were sold to
Mr. Fergusson the architect, who had them entirely
rebuilt and reconstructed.   While the building
was in progress my father took a house in Foley
Place, where we became neighbours of Joseph J.
Hansom, the architect of the Cathedral at Arun-
del.   He was the inventor of the cabs which bear
his name, and founded, or at least originated, the
Builder newspaper.   My father and he became
great friends.   Mr. Hansom was a Roman Catholic,
and my father had become a member of the Church
of England.   The two had frequent and lively
polemical discussions, for my father had studied
theology among other subjects ; but notwithstanding the difference in their faiths, their disputes
were always conducted with temper and moderation.
Among other schools to which I went was one kept
by a Doctor Maclure in Queen Anne Street, on the
same side of the way as, and not far from, J. M.
W. Turner's house.   Maclure was a severe master
and of most irritable nature, using the cane pretty

freely on slight provocation. In hearing the Latin class, if a boy made a false quantity, he would gnash his teeth, and groan "Take the blockhead down!" "Hold out your hand, sir," was his command in extreme cases; and if the delinquent failed to do this, the pedagogue would cut him about the body until the hand was held out to receive the needful punishment. It was the custom, when the school broke up for the holidays, to have examinations of the boys, at which they recited pieces, debates, or dialogues, in English or the classic tongues, for which we were well crammed. The parents and friends of the boys were invited to these displays, which took place at the Institute Rooms in Edward Street, Portman Square. I was in much request on these occasions, as I could "speak up," and was free from nervousness in addressing an audience. I had been cast for a character in a dialogue in Greek, of all languages. I hated the task, as it would have been learning literally by rote what I could not understand, and I succeeded in ridding myself of the odious business in the following way. I had one day a more than usually severe chastise-ment (doubtless well deserved). I took my punish-ment pluckily, and said, "Now, I won't learn that Greek speech; I'll be hanged if I do!" To this mutinous language, oddly enough, the Doctor made no reply. I at once cooled my hand on a school-slate, our sovereign remedy for cuts with the cane, and escaped the speech. The last year of my school-days was passed in the country at Eythorne, a village near Dover. No more canings now; I never saw any corporal punishment. We were "kept in," or had to learn so many lines from a Latin author as punishment, which, in my case, tended to increase my love and veneration for the classics. We had an old French master, a good-natured soul, who never got angry when we laughed at his errors in English or brutally referred to Waterloo. He once went into the shop of the village and asked for a "leetel pork." The attendant showed him some of "our best streaky." "No, no, not zat; I want a leetle pork wiz legs," and we had to assist the Frenchman before the bumpkin intellect could be got to understand that a sucking pig was the desired object.

On returning to Eythorne after the midsummer holidays, for what was to be my last "half" at school, my father gave me a copy of Hugh Clark's "Short and Easy Introduction to Heraldry." It was thought that if I persisted in this love of art now beginning to develop, an outlet for my desire might be found in painting the crests and coats of arms on carriage doors and panels. Heraldry appealed to my budding love of mediævalism, and I studied the book with great zest and interest.

Within a few months I had a fair knowledge of
"the science," and could "blazon a coat" with
readiness and accuracy. But I never became enthusiastic about herald-painting. My first essay
was a crest of a fox argent, courant, regardant, and
after a few others I gave it up altogether.

FONT, SHOREHAM CHURCH.

Looking back on my school-life, I fear I was but
an indifferent scholar; nor did I take more than a
languid interest in cricket or other athletic sports,
the delight of boys of my age. What I enjoyed most
were the country walks on half-holidays, the rambles
in Waldershere Park with its noble trees, or to

Barfrestone and the old Saxon church there, and
now and then a bathe at Deal or Walmer. My
stay here and the occasional trips to Bassingbourne
already mentioned, were all the experiences of
country life I had until I was considerably older,
and it has ever been a matter of regret to me that
I had so little acquaintance with country sounds,
scenes, and occupations in the more impressionable
hours of childhood and early youth.

CHAPTER II

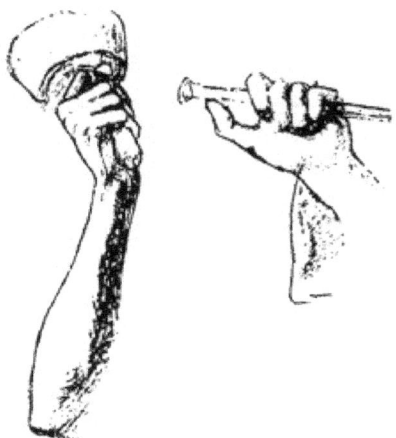

I WAS now fif-
teen, and des-
tined to follow my
father's occupation.
With the view,
therefore, of in-
oculating me with
business-like and
methodical habits,
I attended for
some months at
the place of busi-
ness of a friend of
my father's. I think he was what is called a woollen
warehouse-man. I was set down to an old ledger
or cash-book to add up the amounts of the columns
of figures therein. After some weeks' practice of this
uncongenial pursuit, I had little more facility than
on the day I began. The only relief from this monotonous duty was serving occasionally behind the

16

counter, matching trimmings or selling buttons, known in the trade as "fancy vests."

Meanwhile, the premises described on a former page had changed hands, and become, as I have said, the property of Mr. Fergusson. The Langham Place frontage was displaced by a row of handsome houses (Mocatta, architect), in the centre of which was an entrance to the new business premises, entirely remodelled, and if less picturesque, more convenient, according to the requirements of the day. The place was now known as the London Carriage Repository (Marks & Co.). The business done was chiefly the sale of carriages sent in by makers and dealers, on commission. The actual manufacture had decreased very considerably. Here I passed some years of my life in comparative idleness. The business, always irksome, never enlisted my energy or liking. My duties were simple, consisting chiefly of making out accounts, and waiting on possible or actual customers. Clients they are called in these days of fine English, when a man's house is a residence, his shop an emporium. Once, and once only, I made a sale. Mr. Jacob Bell (the friend of Sir Edwin Landseer), who was an opposite neighbour, came in wanting a gig. I showed him one at twenty guineas. He bought it at once without any question of "lowest price." When I told my father of the transaction, he did not appear to conceive a high idea of my powers as a salesman.

Over the entrance to the Repository was a room, a kind of supplementary office, the walls of which I covered with charcoal drawings, enlarged from Retsch's outlines.   Here in the winter months, after closing hours, I painted heads of our workmen and others by gaslight.   I made a little money by getting a portrait or two now and then, or drawing diagrams for a cousin of mine, J. M. Ashley, who, now in the Church, was then lecturer on chemistry at the Polytechnic close by—an innocent place of entertainment, combining amusement with instruction, the frequenters of which found pleasure in "the exhibition of the diver and the diving-bell," or "General Paisley's plan of exploding gunpowder under water by means of sunken vessels, to be shown below."   Many paid a shilling a head for the delight of descending in the diving-bell, or would throw halfpence to the diver, who, as he rose to the surface of the water, tapped his huge helmet with them in token of their recovery. People were perhaps simpler in those days.   As yet they were ignorant of the intellectual pleasure and refined humour developed by the music-hall— "Most music-'al, most melancholy," as poor Planché used to say.   When about seventeen, I was desirous of attending an art school of an evening, if such could be found. This sounds oddly now, but, if my memory does not deceive me, there were but two private art schools in London at the time—Carey's and Leigh's. It is scarcely incorrect to say there are more art schools to-day than students then. Carey's was more widely known, having been earlier established than Leigh's, but his charges were too high. It must have been through Lance, the fruit-painter, a friend of my father's, and the artist whom I first saw, that Leigh's was discovered. Mr. Dickenson had day-classes for ladies at 18 Maddox Street. The evenings being to let, were taken by some rebellious students of Somerset House, where the National School of Design had been established in 1837. J. R. Herbert, R.A., was, I believe, the leader of the rebellion (regarding the details of which I am ignorant). He was a friend of J. M. Leigh's, who, under his influence, became an art teacher.

I felt nervous and self-conscious in beginning work at Maddox Street; all was new and strange. I had never mixed before with art students, but I soon got on with these, spite of their chaff, and formed with some acquaintances and friendships which have lasted until now. Of these I will only mention H. T. Wells, R.A., H. H. Armstead, R.A., F. Smallfield, of the Old Water Colour Society, and John R. Clayton. It was here I found that I was short-sighted and must take to spectacles when drawing. This reminds me how much more prevalent short-sight must be now than it was forty years ago. I seldom ventured out in my glasses without this sort of thing being said—" Bill! here's a buffer as won't believe his own eyes!" This seems strange and hard of belief, but the statement is none the less true. Now every third person one meets wears a pince-nez, and spectacles are painfully common. I have seen them on the noses of butchers' and bakers' boys—of a street newsvendor, while the number of quite young children, almost babies, in 'barnacles' seems increasing daily.

I will say no more with reference to Maddox Street. All or nearly all my associations and re-collections of "Leigh's" are connected with New-man Street, of which we will say more hereafter.

To return to the Repository. In the year 1850 I find this entry in my diary :—" Ever longing for the day when I can cut business. Rejected as probationer at the Royal Academy." No exclama-tions of sorrow or disappointment, be it observed ; for I always, after destroying a very early diary, in which I found opinions recorded that verged on idiotcy, resolved for the future to record facts rather than sentiments. In the following year I was more fortunate. My father allowed me three days a week off for study, and in December

1851 I succeeded in becoming a student of the Royal Academy.

Affairs had not been going well lately—indeed, for some time past. I feel, not without a twinge of sadness, that my father, with much shrewdness and common-sense in most matters, had not the faculty for business. He might perhaps have prospered in the law, for he had, as it seemed to me, many qualifications of the legal mind. Be that as it may, he came to grief, and the carriage repository, which had been for some time in the market, was finally sold. I was now—February 1852—free, and worked each day at the Academy schools, going to Leigh's of an evening. Before my father's affairs became so much involved, he would talk of allowing me fifty guineas a year to start me on my own account, but this never came off.

Mr. Fergusson had commissioned Mr. Dibdin, a clever scene-painter and water-colourist, to paint a panorama of the Ganges for him. This was exhibited for a while in Regent Street, opposite the Polytechnic, but removed subsequently to Leicester Square, where Mr. Fergusson engaged me (through my father) as checktaker for four hours a day at thirty shillings a week. But the panorama did not catch on ; "'twas caviare to the general." " Paper " was plentiful, but money scarce. The panorama ceased to draw. At the end of the first week it was closed, and from that day to this I have never seen my thirty shillings.

Let us leave Langham Place and its attendant troubles, and turn to Newman Street at No. 79, where James Mathews Leigh kept his art school; open all day from 6 to 6, and again from 7 to 10 in the evening. I have already mentioned how I first met my art master and future friend at Maddox Street. Between then and the Newman Street period, I met him in another capacity. It was the year of the great Chartist scare, 1848. It was said that two hundred thousand men were to assemble on Kennington Common, march thence to West-minster, and present a monster petition, which was to be carried in cabs to the House of Commons. The Bank and other public establishments were occupied by the military, and one hundred and fifty thousand people of all ranks and conditions were enrolled as special constables. The late Em-peror of the French, Napoleon the Third, was one, and Leigh and I were enrolled. The head-quarters of the Marylebone division were at the National Schools in Riding-House Lane, by All Souls' Church, and here I found Leigh, who must have been about forty years of age, looking smart in a tightly buttoned frock-coat, clean shaven, and very upright. He was a strongly built man, with good broad forehead, a piercing eye, square jaw, and

J. M. LEIGH, WHEN GROWING HIS BEARD.

thin lips, with a look of great firmness and determination. My father kept the doors of his premises
closed on the dreaded day, the 10th of April, thinking, if the infuriated Chartists got the upper hand,
they might make barricades of our carriages across
Portland Place. But his fears, like many others
on that day, proved to be groundless. The two
hundred thousand dwindled to twenty thousand;
the military were not called out, and the day passed
quietly enough, and I neither heard of or saw any
incident more serious than the chaff and ridicule
of knots of people directed against the "specials"
who patrolled the district, each one with a stout
staff, and wearing a wristlet as distinctive badge.

I worked for many years at Leigh's, on and off,
sometimes in the day as well as at night, and
sometimes before breakfast. There must have
been some affinity between us, for we became
firm and fast friends, and many were the acts of
kindness Leigh showed towards me, which shall
be mentioned presently. He was called "Dagger
Leigh," not for carrying concealed arms, but
from the habit he had of making cynical remarks
and sarcastic repartees. I have heard he could
hold his own with Thackeray and Jerrold. He
was a cousin of Charles Mathews, the inimitable
comedian. No mean actor himself, I have often
seen him give impersonations of Mazzini, the

political agitator, walking up and down the gallery
with rapid strides among the casts from the
antique and the easels, with impassioned gesture,
rolling out sarcasm and invective in "very choice

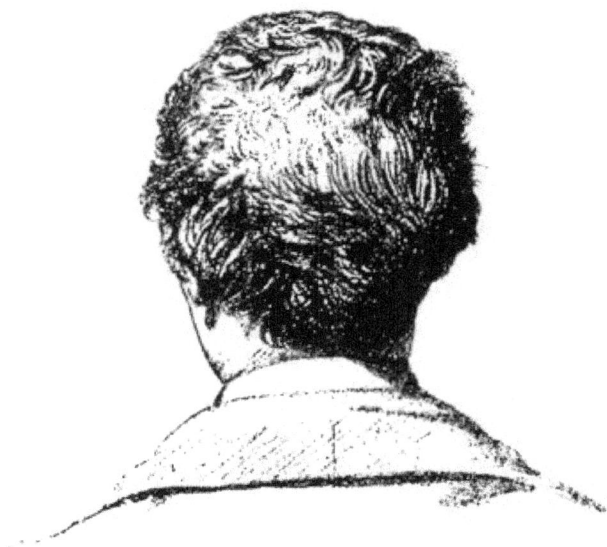

BACK OF MY HEAD, SKETCHED BY J. M. LEIGH.

Italian," for he was a good linguist, and had spent
much of his early life on the Continent.   In working hours Leigh wore a skull-cap and a long loose
kind of gaberdine of black velvet, and smoked a

clay pipe, a moderately lengthy "churchwarden."
In teaching he had no regular method or system,
leaving us pretty much to our own devices. Sometimes he would take palette and brushes from a
student, and with a few strokes show him how
to indicate a head or limb on the margin of
his canvas. Or something which struck him
in one of our studies supplied a text for an
impromptu lecture on "surface," "regions," or
"masses," as we should call them, or other subject,
on which he would discourse with shrewd common-
sense and frequent touches of fun. He was a great
stickler for cleanliness and tidiness. "Keep your
palette as clean as your breakfast-table," he would
say,—"a much easier thing than to get your breakfast by your palette." Under all the cynicism there
was a kind and generous nature. By my absenting
myself for some time, attending only the weekly
sketching meetings, he thought perhaps I was more
than usually hard up, and took an opportunity of
slipping into my hand a paper on which he had
written, "Come for nothing, as a little Christmas
present." I was painting my second picture of
"Hamlet, Horatio, and Osric." I had shown him
the sketch, in which Hamlet was dressed in a long
robe with hanging sleeves. He said nothing; had
the dress made, lent it to me for as long as I
wanted it, and then had it placed in the costume

wardrobe. As we got on, and began to try our luck at the Academy, Leigh encouraged us to take our pictures on a stated evening before " sending in day," when they would be arranged in single file along the gallery, and he, still smoking the perennial pipe, would pass from one to another, criticising, lecturing, and suggesting improvements.

Joseph Clark brought his celebrated picture of "The Sick Child" on one of these evenings. We were all struck with wonder by its technique, its pathos, its human nature. No one suspected that Clark, so quiet and retiring, could produce such a work, for at the sketching meetings, at the end of the two hours, when time was up, he would have little more than a head, or sometimes a figure, slightly but always charmingly indicated. There was the picture in answer to our doubts—but in what a state! covered with hairs from brushes, dust, and other impurities. Leigh, who always inculcated that a clean workmanlike "surface" was one of the essentials of a picture, took a palette knife, daintily detached the excrescences, and washed and oiled the picture, much to the improvement both of surface and appearance.

For some years before his death, Leigh used to ask a few of his older students to sup with him in batches of two or three at a time. He was a widower: the household consisted of his mother, a Mathews by birth, a chatty, lively old lady, with a sense of humour and plenty of anecdote, and his only son, Henry S. Leigh (whom I first knew as a Bluecoat-boy), who had much of his father's talent for repartee, and was a good and witty versifier. His " Carols of Cockayne" were well known to the last, if not to the present generation. Artists lived far simpler lives forty years ago, and the fare on these evenings consisted of little more than bread and cheese with table-beer, and a " smiler " or "refresher " of gin and water, with the smoke after supper. Wit presided at the board and made brilliant the banquet. Leigh was an admirable talker rather than a conversationalist, but we were all willing listeners. When not in the vein for discourse, cards were introduced, and old-fashioned round games played, or table-turning, for which Leigh had lately developed a craze, would be resorted to.

The more prominent figures whom I used to meet at these symposia were T. J. Heatherley, grave of aspect but quietly humorous ; John Sparkes, with whom I first became acquainted when drawing at the British Museum, now headmaster at South Kensington. Leigh called us Box and Cox, from the similarity of our names. In addition were J. F. Slinger, lately one of the masters at the Slade School, University College, a pianist who played with taste and feeling ; and E. W. Russell, whom we shall meet again. These two with H. Leigh, who was no mean pianist, contributed to the harmony of the evening when music was wished for. Walter Thornbury must not be forgotten, an excitable, impulsive, careless man, who worked hard at the antique, but in a perfunctory manner, for his mind was occupied while drawing with thoughts of how to turn a phrase or compose a couplet. He soon had the good sense to see that art was not his vocation (he gave six toes to a foot of the Gladiator), and the opportunity offering, he wrote a series of articles on the Courts of the Sydenham Crystal Palace, then in course of completion, for publication in the *Athenæum*, of which journal he eventually, under the editorship of Hepworth Dixon, became art critic. His " Old London ", was, I believe, fairly successful ; less known was a volume of verse, " Songs of the Cavaliers and Roundheads," for which I made some half-dozen illustrations. His " Life of J. M. W. Turner " was carelessly written and failed to make any mark.

I cannot resist breaking off here to relate an experience which, though not intimately connected with my studies in drawing, was not without its influence, in an artistic sense, on my future tastes and proclivities. It made a great impression on

me at the time, and is inextricably mixed up with
my Newman Street memories.

It was not until I had been at Leigh's some
little time that I entered a theatre. Surprising as
this statement may appear, it must be remembered
that I had been strictly brought up, and taught to
look on a theatre as a temple of sin, to be shunned
by all good boys and girls. An old school-fellow
called one evening for me at Newman Street, as
he wished to have my advice on some subject
which could only be told to my private ear. He
asked if I would take a walk with him ; we presently found ourselves near what was then called
the Queen's Theatre in Tottenham Street, an
obscure enough place then, since made famous
under the management of the Bancrofts. At the
time of which I write, it was irreverently termed
the Royal Pill-Box or the Royal Dust-Hole, the
former title in allusion to its size, the latter, I pre-
sume, because its pretensions to cleanliness were
not conspicuous. The evening was sufficiently
advanced for the hour of half-price to have begun.
My friend proposed we should enter. Curiosity
having been aroused, I required little persuasion,
and in we went. Here indeed was a new world
to me ; it seemed a compendium of all the fairy
tales I had ever read, the " Arabian Nights," and
Scott's novels. At this distance of time I well

remember the actor and the speech he uttered. A bravo with the conventional boots, buckled belt, and pistols was addressing a group of men who had apparently been uttering disparaging remarks on him. " You know me ! " he shouted, " know me as what ? Cuzique the bold and daring, Cuzique the rover, the pirate if you will, but not Cuzique the coward. My step, you see, is light." With that he folded his arms, eyed his traducers from head to foot, and crossed the stage, making the boards tremble as he strode them with inter-jectional stops between each stride. I had little time to see more than a scene or so of the next piece, which was the "Ship of Glass," for I was due at home from Leigh's at about half-past ten. Staying till the last moment I dared, I ran home (we lived in Mornington Road then). My father opened the door to me. " You're late," was all he said, but he had a manner of saying things when he was cross that was harder to endure than a good box of the ear would have been, and I sat down to my frugal supper of bread and cheese with half a pint of porter, uncomfortable and abashed.

I saw Cuzique often after this ; he was the heavy man of the company. His name was E. Green. One Boxing Night he was playing in a piece before the pantomime. The part was a very heavy one. He was grunting, groaning, and with one hand in his bosom doing that "business" known as "searching for the flea." The audience were impatient for the fun of the pantomime to begin, and were getting noisy. At length, when Green gave vent to a still greater groan of agony, a voice shouted from the gallery, " Bring it up, old man! why don't you get a basin ?"

I continued to work of an evening at Leigh's till within a year or so of his death, and enjoyed his friendship to the last. But a few days before he died we took our Academy work for his inspection. He had for some time been suffering from a painful disease—smoker's cancer in the lips or tongue. He bore it with great patience and fortitude. I can see him now—the lower part of his face enveloped in a white silk handkerchief, the broad shoulders a little bent, the tread no longer firm and elastic, as he moved from one picture to another, nodding or shaking his head, which, with gestures of the hand, were all he could do in the way of criticism now. It was sad to see the vigorous energetic man who loved to talk, walking silently among the works of his pupils and to know his days were numbered. He was relieved of his pains and found rest on the 20th April 1860, at the comparatively early age of fifty-two. A numerous band of his students followed him to his grave in Highgate Cemetery.

Leigh was a pupil of Etty, and painted historic and religious subjects. He exhibited at the Academy and elsewhere from 1825 to 1849 inclusive. It was as a portrait-painter that he was most successful. I have seen portraits by him, brilliant in effect and vigorous in handling, which might bear comparison with the works of Jackson, the friend of Haydon, Chantrey, and Sir George Beaumont. From the time of his father's death I saw less and less of Harry Leigh, as our paths in life diverged. Now and then I spent evenings at his chambers in Furnival's Inn with him and other choice spirits, Thornbury, John Hollingshead, Jeffery Prowse, and Godfrey Turner being of the number.

Later we were members of a small club called "The Circle," from its embracing votaries of all the arts—young journalists, actors, singers, painters, and sculptors. One of the number, Edward Draper, gave us our motto, "Totus teres atque rotundus." We were Bohemian and nomadic. Having no settled habitation, we met at rooms in taverns, generally in the neighbourhood of Covent Garden. Other members were Val Prinsep, Ouless, E. A. Waterlow, E. Buckman, Byron Webber, Irving Montague, war correspondent, pictorial and literary, Hain Friswell, Storey, P. R. Morris, Alfred Parsons, &c. &c.

H. S. Leigh would sometimes at our meetings

sit down to the piano, and, accompanying himself,
troll out his own compositions, "The Twins,"
"Uncle John," with much vivacity and go. The
club has ceased to exist some years. I find no

THE MISER.

trace of it after 1879 or 1880. It came to grief
through absurd jealousy among some of the
members, the details of which I am pleased to
think I have entirely forgotten.

Harry Leigh, as he was always called by his intimates, died on the 16th June 1883, at an earlier age than his father, being only forty-six. Edward Draper told me "Leigh was to have met me by appointment one Saturday evening at the Savage Club. On my way thither I saw, to my great sorrow, 'Death of Mr. H. S. Leigh' on the contents bill of an evening newspaper."

The art school at 79 Newman Street still exists. After Leigh's death it was carried on for many years by T. J. Heatherley, and is now under the mastership of a relative of my old fellow-student.

CHAPTER III

1852

ON the morning of January 29, 1852, I met Calderon at the steam - boat wharf by London Bridge, to start for Paris *viâ* Boulogne. For sometime Calderon, who had stayed there before, often urged me to go over, and would speak of the superiority of the teaching to be had there to any then obtainable in London, the advantage of working among students, each one of whom drew better than oneself, &c., &c. I was quite eager to go, and was only prevented by want of funds. These were supplied eventually by one or two generous friends. So we embarked at an early hour that winter morning, while yet scarcely daylight. I remember little of the passage beyond the fact that both of us went below at once, and

were before long sympathetically sea-sick.   It was
dark by the time we reached Boulogne, and the
railway journey seemed as though it would never
end, though I suppose we slept a little.   We got to

CALDERON.

Paris at some frightfully early hour, drove to the
lodging which a friend, an Irishman named Bland,
was to have secured for us, but had failed somehow
to get : so there was nothing to do but leave our

CALDERON.

luggage, and walk about the streets until such hour as we could venture to knock up Bland. He opened his room door in his night-shirt, and though but half awake, gave us a most genial and hearty welcome. As soon as he was dressed, he went out for milk and other comestibles, and while he made the coffee, Calderon and I got rid of some dust and dirt, and we breakfasted merrily together. The meal over, the first thing was to go out, the first place to see, the Louvre. On our way I noticed many houses the walls of which were covered with bullet-marks and abrasions, suggestive of the recent *coup d'état*. After some hours passed in the Louvre, and having got a lodging, we were ready for more pictures, and visited the Luxembourg, then dined, and finished a pretty long day by going to the theatre at night and seeing Mlle. Dejazet in some piece in which she played the part of a rakish young man. She was then not over sixty summers, I believe.

Our lodging consisted of but one room in a house in the Rue des Martyrs, in the Montmartre quarter, and near the Atelier Picot, where I hoped to study. In this room for nearly five months Calderon and I lived together in perfect amity, poor but content. We shared the same bed, dined at the same restaurant, and were, as much from inclination as from motives of economy, inseparable. We soon called on M. Picot at his private house. He was a little, spare, snuffy man, in skull-cap and spectacles, working on large cartoons of apostles nine or ten feet high, for the decoration of a Parisian church (Notre Dame des Lorettes). He received me very graciously, and having signified his assent to my becoming one of his pupils, we took our departure, and proceeded to the neighbouring atelier. I was soon made aware of its vicinity by a great noise of laughter mingled with shouting and singing. On entering, Calderon was noisily welcomed on his return, while they crowded around me as if I were a specimen of some savage tribe, and criticised my personal appearance with a candour that might have aroused my anger had I been less ignorant of French. The atelier was a large square room, lighted by a skylight, bare of furniture save easels and rush-covered stools. A good-sized throne for models stood in the centre, at one end was a slightly raised platform for those students who painted or who preferred easels and a longer view. The majority worked on the floor proper on low stools, with a taller one on which to rest their portfolios; for drawing-boards, tacks, or strained paper were unknown. Papier Ingrès was universally employed, and a sheet of this pinned to the portfolio. In one corner of the room was a solitary antique figure—the Germanicus. The walls had

for their only decoration two rows of paintings—
one of studies from the life, the other of original
sketches, chiefly classical and biblical.   These were
executed by present or past students, and were
plainly framed by strips of wood, with the author's
name below.   One bore the name of Bougereau,
and I was glad to see that of a compatriot, John
Cross, appended to another.

The duties of the *nouveau* or last-comer were
simple and not too arduous.   He was expected
to look after the stove-fire, to run errands, and to
act as general fag.   Once I was sent to the house
of the master after atelier hours, and, assisted by
an old and favourite model of his, had to prick
the outline of the large apostles already referred to
for "pouncing" on to the church wall.   But as his
very first duty, the *nouveau* was expected to stand
a bowl of punch or *vin chaud*, and sing a song or
make a speech before he was free of the atélier.
The punch was soon obtained, and I "scored" by
crying "Vive la belle France," as I took off my
glass.   A speech with my very limited vocabulary
being out of the question, I sang them the old song
of "Guy Fawkes" with its chorus of "Bow-wow."
This was so new and incomprehensible to them
that they were fairly "knocked."   At once the
relations between us became friendly, and I went
by the name of "Bow-wow" for several weeks.

The fact of my being a foreigner and understanding so little of their language told greatly in my favour with regard to the students' treatment of me; but the *nouveau*, if a Frenchman, or more especially a Parisian, was tormented and persecuted to a degree which in some cases was little if at all short of brutal. There was a cellar reached by a trap-door under part of the atelier floor. Into this the luckless *nouveau* would be sometimes conducted, will he, nill he, when he would have squibs and crackers thrown in on him from above, and subsequently, lest possibly his clothes should catch fire, drenched with water! At other times the luckless youth would be "crucified," as they called it. This consisted in tying him securely by his head and limbs to a ladder, and, preceded by one of their number blowing on an old hunting-horn, he was borne by four students along the suburb, the remainder following in solemn procession. Now and then ladder and *nouveau* would be placed against some convenient blank wall, and left there for a while, exposed to the jeers and laughter of the passers-by.

One day was much like another at the Atelier Picot. The model would sit soon after 8 A.M.; at 6 in the summer months. After two hours' work an interval of half an hour was allowed for breakfast. We all went outside the Barrier for this, everything being cheaper there than inside. The wealthier would have a "bifstek" at a restaurant, but most of us brought our bread and a sausage or so, or some fruit as the season advanced. This frugal meal was washed down by a drink of water from the atélier *fontaine*. I should not care to drink that water now, but we had the confidence of youth and had never heard of bacteria or bacilli.

After breakfast the model would resume the pose for another two hours. He or she had to make up the regulation four hours exclusive of rests. Occasionally we clubbed sous together and got the model to sit after the regular hours. Thus a good morning's work had been got through, yet it was still early in the day. Some would remain longer at the atélier sketching each others' portraits, others would go to copy at the Louvre or work at home. After a few weeks I was admitted student of the Ecole des Beaux Arts, and would draw there in the afternoon. I was struck with the difference of time allowed for probationership at the Ecole and at our own Royal Academy. There it occupied a week only. At the Academy in my time it lasted three months. Certainly the French who contested for the studentship were more advanced in their studies than my fellow-probationers at the Academy. At the Ecole only one drawing had to be made, and that from the life.

The model sat two clear hours each morning

for six days.   Perfect silence was enforced, and at the close of the sitting all drawings were collected, placed in a portfolio and put away till the following morning, when the drawings were given out again to the competitors.

There were monthly *concours* at Picot's, to which many of the pupils would send their drawings or paintings from life, and sketches of a uniform size of any subject they might fancy.   No prizes were given in these competitions, numbers only being awarded by the master in order of merit.   Calderon and I resolved to go in for the sketch competition, and stayed at our room one bitter cold day to make it.   We went to the expense of a fire for that occasion only; ordinarily we sat and shivered in our great-coats when "at home."   Calderon took a scene from one of Byron's poems for his subject, and I " Christ Disputing with the Doctors."   I forget what numbers we obtained.   Calderon's sketch was brilliant and full of go, but when I think of my own even at this time, I have a cold shudder!   As spring came on, we now and then did a little outdoor sketching by the Buttes Montmartre.   We dined at a very cheap restaurant in the Rue Molière, going afterwards to an evening life-school—a school without a master, kept by an ex-model named Boudin, of whom I remember nothing except that he was "fat and scant of breath," and a most inordinate smoker of long thin-stemmed clay-pipes, in the colouring of which he took great pride. There was a legend current that he smoked as he slept in his bed. After Boudin's was over, we ended the day by walking home, and being fairly tired by the time we got there, went at once to bed and sleep.

The first Sunday morning in Paris I dutifully went to the English church in the Rue d'Agnesseau. I expect I was a little home-sick, though I had left home so recently ; the sight of the English faces, the sound of English voices, gave me much pleasure, but a pleasure dearly purchased at 1 fr. 25 c. for a seat. I never repeated my visit. We tried one or two evening services at a French Protestant chapel, but found the place close and stuffy, and the service somniferous, and soon discontinued our attendance. We much preferred roaming about the city with Bland, looking in at different churches for the enjoyment of the music, or loafing about the squares and gardens, or taking a suburban walk to enjoy the pure fresh air, the blue sky, and brilliant sunshine. Sunshine without and sunshine within warmed us in those delightful Paris days, before the battle of life had begun, when hope was high and care unknown !

Among the students at Picot's with whom I worked were Leon Perrault, who has since made his mark as a painter, and Gustave Droz, who,

forsaking art for literature, became a successful
novelist.

BELGIUM

1860

In the spring of the year 1860, Mr. Mudie took
a party composed of two Dissenting ministers,
Smallfield, of the Old Water Colour Society,
and myself for a little foreign tour. One of these
ministers was Mr. Mudie's father-in-law, a kind-
hearted old gentleman with a sunny nature; the
other a much younger man, named Graham, suc-
cessor to Doctor Leifchild at Craven Chapel.
It might appear an oddly assorted party, but
we got on very harmoniously. Mr. Mudie paid
all expenses of the journey, including those
of living and sight-seeing. We had a courier,
too, who spoke the most wonderful polyglot.
"Quel wein is dat?" I once heard him ask a
waiter. We visited that delightful trio of picturesque old towns, Ghent, Bruges, and Antwerp.
Thence to Holland, making brief stays at Rotter-
dam; the Hague, with its splendid Rembrandts
and over-rated Paul Potter; Leyden, where we
went over the nurseries of a florist with the Shakespearian name of Rosencrantz, who had many fine
varieties of tulips and quantities of feathered

hyacinths; and Amsterdam, where we stayed a
Sunday. As the reverend gentlemen had no objection, we went to the Zoo, where I admired the
fine collection of flamingoes and the way they were
housed. It was here we saw a very fat Dutch-
man of very excitable nature, who kept shouting,
" Paauw! paauw!" at sight of the peacock. Our
holiday ended with a trip on the Rhine between
Cologne and Mayence. And a most enjoyable holiday it was, and all were sorry when it came to an
end. I find this record of it in my diary: "This
journey confirmed me in love of the art, and the
determination, if possible, to quit the monotonous
drudgery of drawing for glass."

Three years later, in company with Yeames and
Hodgson, I revisited Belgium. We had letters of
introduction from Yeames's merchant brother to a
Monsieur David Verbist, one of the "great ones of
the city" of Antwerp. It struck us as somewhat
odd, on entering the outer office, to find the clerks
writing letters or adding up the columns of their
ledgers with the soothing accompaniment of a
cigar. Ushered into the presence of the principal,
we found him also smoking. He received us very
kindly, and at once offered us cigars. The walls
of his office were literally lined with drawers and
lockers containing thousands of cigars of all the
best varieties of brand. We dined with Mr.

Verbist on one or two occasions. He lived in the actual house which had belonged, so it was said, to Rubens. I had heard that "on mange bien en Belgique," and the dinner was plentiful and *recherché*. Plenty of plate on the table and side-boards, and by the side of each guest's cover was placed a little silver rest on which to place the knife and fork between the courses, for these were not supposed to be changed during the meal.

The conversation naturally turned on art and the Belgian painters. Our host spoke with reverential awe of Baron Henri Leys—how he would like to have one of his pictures, but didn't quite see his way—"the Baron was a difficult man to approach." This was a difficulty which we comparatively im-pecunious painters did not share with the rich merchant. We had an introduction to, and called upon, the great man, for he had a European repu-tation, and we the greatest respect and admiration for his artistic powers. Leys received us at once in the most genial way, handed us cigars, treating us *en camarade*, and talking as if he were but a student. He showed us his dining-room, the walls of which were decorated with paintings illustrating a banquet, the arrival and departure of the guests, &c. Small replicas of these were exhibited in the London International Exhibition of 1862. I regret that I can recall little if any of his conversation, but have a lively remembrance of the hearty aversion with which he spoke of all Academies and academic teaching. On leaving Leys, after a somewhat prolonged call, we strolled out to the old fortifications of the town, built by Vauban, no vestige of which now remains. Here, seated on the grass, and warmed by the genial sunshine of spring, we discussed at length all the incidents of our visit, with the appearance and sayings of the painter Baron.

Other artists whom we called on were De Keyser, the president of the Belgian Academy, Verlat, the animal painter, and Van Lerius, who talked in so excitable a manner that we dubbed him De Lirious. He asked had we been to Ghent to see " L'Agneau Pascal" by Van Eyck. " Mon Dieu," he cried, " c'est magnifique—c'est étonnant —c'est à se mettre aux genoux devant." But he did not rhapsodise on Leys. "Ah oui! c'est un beau talent, mais il manque des études sérieuses ! "

Rubens is the presiding genius of Antwerp, yet, with every admiration of his great and daringly original talent, it is quite possible to have too much of him, as of any good thing. In going round the churches, those pictures which the guides are not sufficiently barefaced to attribute to that fecund master gain a reflected glory in being by " Pietro Pourbus, master (of) Rubens." On returning of an evening to our hotel in the Place Verte, where there is a clumsy statue of the painter, I would uncover my head, and bending low on one knee, cry aloud, "Hommage à toi, Rubens, le plus grand peintre du monde!" Despite my reverential manner, *les braves Belges* regarded me either as *un grand farceur* or a harmless lunatic.

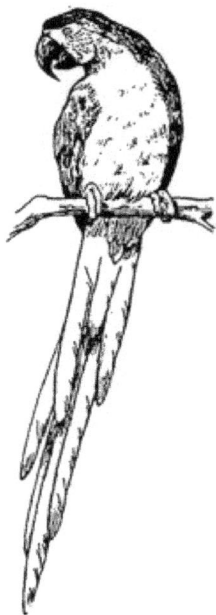

CHAPTER IV

AFTER PARIS—CLAYTON AND BELL— DUBLIN

1853-1859

I RETURNED from Paris in the middle of June 1852, having studied less than five months there, but made good use of that short time and was fairly industrious. Meanwhile my father had emigrated to Australia in the hope of retrieving his fallen fortunes. I found my mother and three brothers living in the upper part of a house in John Street, Bedford Row.

I at once rejoined Leigh's, and soon began my first picture, a single half-length figure of Dogberry. This was sent to the British Institution in the beginning of 1853. With many other students, I was much influenced by the Pre-Raphaelite School, and that influence was very evident in the picture. "The lay element," the noblemen and gentlemen amateurs who formed the greater section of the selecting committee of that Institution, were perhaps not favourably disposed to the new movement in art. Anyhow they rejected Dogberry. But I didn't lose heart, and in due time sent it to the Academy, where, to my great delight, it was both accepted and hung. In those days outsiders were not, as now, allowed a whole day for varnishing and touching, but a few hours only on the morning of the day when the Exhibition was opened to the public. My joy was increased by finding my picture well placed in the West Room, immediately below "the line," next to Holman Hunt's "Strayed Sheep," and I had the additional satisfaction of hearing that artist say to a friend, "Who painted that? It isn't bad."

The sale of an artist's first picture, like the memory of his first love, endures through life, and I cannot resist giving an account of how my earliest patron and I came together.

I had not been long at work one morning in

the beginning of May when a fellow-student named Rainford called and asked, "What price will you take for 'Dogberry'? Ten pounds?" I thought this sum too low (I asked twenty-five pounds), and would rather wait for a better offer. "Well, fifteen pounds? You can have the money at once if you like." This decided me. "I'll take the offer," cried I. "Come along!" said he. We then lived in Holborn, and hurrying out, hailed a passing 'bus going Citywards, and in a brief space of time were in the office of Mr. Christie, a stockbroker of Copthall Chambers. His reception was frank and hearty. But a few years my senior, he was unlike all my preconceived ideas of a patron. He wrote out the cheque at once, and asked us to lunch with him at his office. This we did after I had got the cheque changed into gold. In the evening our host treated Rainford and me to a performance at the Victoria Theatre of the fine old melodramatic type. I think the piece was called "The Dog of Montargis." "Brayvo Hicks" was the hero, and a live dog, who was continually alluded to as "this poor dumb ber-rute," was one of the performers. After this, still at our host's expense, we supped at Rouget's restaurant in the neighbourhood of Leicester Square—long since demolished. The day's excitement over, I went home and to bed, but not before I had carefully placed the fifteen new sovereigns on a table where my mother could not fail to see them in the morning. For several years after the sale of "Dogberry," I continued painting, at rare intervals selling a picture, doing any wood-drawing that came in my way, or portraits at a pound or thirty shillings a piece—living, in fact, from hand to mouth. At this time there was an institution for the exhibition and sale of pictures called the Portland Gallery, opposite the Polytechnic in Regent Street, which was very serviceable to young artists, as, if their work was not too glaringly bad, they could reckon with all but absolute certainty on its being seen by the public. There was a selecting committee, but its judgments were distinguished by leniency rather than severity. By paying at the rate of one guinea per superficial foot, an exhibitor was entitled to the space he required not only on the line, but above and below it. These fees and the commissions on sales paid the working expenses. The exhibition could not be called first-rate, though some good men were among the contributors—notably Robert Scott Lauder, the teacher of Pettie, Orchardson, &c. Here I sold some few pictures, two of them being bought by the late W. J. Broderip, the magistrate and naturalist. He had chambers in Raymond's Buildings, Gray's Inn, to which he once

invited me. The walls were covered with pictures,
hung so closely together that it was impossible to
see whether they concealed panelling or paper.
But of all those pictures, the only one which remains
in my memory is "The Hireling Shepherd," by
Holman Hunt. But sales of pictures were not
sufficiently frequent to enable one to dispense with
any way of making the pot boil. Some wood-
drawing came in unexpectedly. There was a
periodical known as the *Home Circle*, in which
a history of Turkey and Russia, written by John
Oxenford, appeared from week to week. It was the
time of the Crimean war. I had to make one illustration for each number. The first two blocks were
wanted in a great hurry. I hastened straightway
to the Reading-Room of the British Museum to
get some notions of costume, &c., for I was as
ignorant on all such points as the babe unborn; and
by dint of sitting up half the night contrived to
perform the allotted task by the time it was needed.
The editor was Pierce Egan, junior, the son of
the author of "Life in London," in which the fast
life of Tom and Jerry and their "Corinthian"
friends is recorded with a most lavish use of italics.
My work did not satisfy my editor, and I seldom
went to the office without his going to a bureau,
when, bringing out a pile of numbers of the *London
Journal*, he would point to Sir John (then plain

Mr.) Gilbert's brilliant designs, and say, "There! that's the kind of thing we want—more variety of line—the thick and the thin." I complied with this as far as I was able, studied Sir John's cuts again and again, and even cribbed whole figures from them when I saw any that might be adapted; but this was all I could do. Doubtless my drawings were bad, but the price paid for them was not high. I got but ten shillings a block, and had to find my own wood. The engraver must have been propor- tionately remunerated, for he hacked and slashed my work in such a way as to make the last state of those blocks considerably worse than the first. When, years after, I related my experience to Sir J. Gilbert, he said, "Ah! yes; when I went round to the pub- lishers, I was told to draw as much as possible in the manner of William Harvey, who was the reign- ing fashion then." The *Home Circle* became de- funct in about six months, but I believe the collapse was not so much owing to my illustrations, as to certain financial difficulties with the publisher—at least that was my impression, though I cannot vouch for the fact. I next find myself at some Literary Institute as "Professor" of Drawing (save the mark). If I had not written evidence of this, I should feel inclined to doubt it, for I entirely forget the name of the Institute, and that of the street where it was situated. The duties were light. I devoted two evenings a week to a class strong in enthusiasm, but feeble in number. The fees were at the rate of so much a head. When my first (and last) quarter was over, I found myself the richer by something under two pounds. It was scarcely good enough, so I resigned. A young, ardent, but impecunious friend of mine succeeded me. If I remember rightly, he also resigned, but did not wait till the end of his quarter to take that step.

In the year 1856 I had a small picture at the Royal Academy called "Toothache in the Middle Ages." It was the means of a "sell" by which I was completely taken in. We were still living (my mother and three brothers) in Holborn; a few doors westward was a dentist named André Fresco, who had at the door of his establishment one of those ghastly waxen masks which drops its jaw at stated intervals, now showing a row of bare gums, now a set of teeth of a whiteness and brilliancy which Nature happily can never rival.

The picture was nearly finished, and "sending in day" approaching, when one morning I received a letter, purporting to come from the dentist, half in English, half in French, in which the writer said he had heard of the work—thought it *spirituelle* and witty in idea, and would like to become its fortunate possessor. Not content with this, he would be glad if I would paint him a companion picture,

"No Toothache in the Nouveau Siècle," for which
Monsieur A. F. would pose as model as the good
génie apportant le remède.   I was simple enough
to be taken in with this, and replied that, flattered
as I was by his appreciation and wishes to have my
work, I would like him to see the picture before
sending it to the Royal Academy.   I shortly received a curt note in a bold business hand, so different from the dainty writing of the first letter.
"Mr. André Fresco knows nothing about the
picture referred to," was all it said.   I referred
to that first letter, and found it bore the date of
April 1 !

I soon discovered this trick had been played
on me by a cousin, then George, now Sir George
Buchanan, late Medical Officer of Health of the
Local Government Board.   The Exhibition opened,
and one morning shortly afterwards my mother
called me down-stairs from the little room which
served as a studio at the top of the house.   On
entering the dining-room, I found a kind-hearted,
pleasant-looking man, whose face did not belie his
nature, for he had come straight from the Academy,
having been pleased with the "Toothache," and
wishing to have it.   There being no obstacles in
the way, he took it at the price asked, and sent a
cheque the next day.   His name was Charles
Edward Mudie, founder of the world-famed library

known as "Mudie's." It was the first time I had seen Mr. Mudie, but found that he and my mother were already acquainted, for they were talking on matters connected with Dissent and Dissenters, with which both were familiar. But we became firm friends afterwards, and Mr. Mudie subsequently bought another picture of mine, "Dogberry's Charge to the Watch," in the Academy of 1859. Both pictures remain in the family, and when I last saw them before the illness and death of Mr. Mudie, both were in perfect preservation, without a crack and looking as if painted but yesterday.

Besides "Toothache," mentioned above, I sold a picture that season to Mr. Broderip at the Portland, "The Gravedigger's Riddle," from "Hamlet" —"What is he that builds stronger than either the mason, the shipwright, or the carpenter?"—a composition of two figures with a background painted from the porch in Stoke Pogis Churchyard, where Gray is supposed to have written the celebrated "Elegy." This double success emboldened me to get married, which event took place at St. George's Church, Bloomsbury, in the quietest manner, without parade or fuss, which we did not wish nor our means warrant. After a fortnight at Bristol and Clifton, we returned to town, and began housekeeping at rooms in Tonbridge Place, part of the Euston (then called the New) Road. The first

picture painted here was a full-length figure of
"Bottom enacting Pyramus," from the "Midsummer
Night's Dream"—an unfortunate picture from the
first. It was skied in the West Room of the R.A.,
and looking at the work since, I wonder it was not
rejected at once! It was *too* ugly. Sent to every
provincial exhibition in the kingdom, crossing the
Atlantic to America, where it was shown at Boston,
it still came back to me. No dog was ever so
faithful in persistent devotion to its owner as this
picture to me. I have it now, but carefully concealed from the eye of man. Christie's shall never
know it!

Working at home all day, either painting or
drawing on wood, I used now to go to Langham
Chambers of an evening, where there was a Society
of Artists who met for the study of the nude or
draped model in alternate weeks. Formerly its
meeting-place was in a sculptor's yard in Clipstone
Street. Sir John Tenniel was one of the artists
who worked here. When I joined the Society, it
had not very long migrated to larger and more
commodious premises in All Souls Place (a small
street on the northern side of the church), on the
ground-floor of the house known as Langham
Chambers. Mr. Lowes Dickenson then and still
occupies rooms in the upper part. So did Luard,
an artist who began life as a military man, was

in the Crimean war, and died when still young.
W. Gale, still living, I am glad to say, was another
occupant. Of these chambers W. W. Deane was
the architect, and arranged all with due regard to
economy of space and constructive simplicity. The
Artists' Society have two principal rooms, besides
others. On the ground-floor a large studio, with
the usual platform for posing, and a great gasalier
for lighting the model; rails run around, with small
gas jets at intervals, for the convenience of those
working. Those who used easels stood outside
the rails. The room next in size has a good
library of art works and a long table in its centre.
The model finished the sitting an hour earlier on
Friday evenings, that all might be clear for the
great feature of Langham—the sketching night.
Two subjects, one landscape, the other figure, were
chosen, and announced on a slate the week before.
After coffee had been served, the sketchers set to
work. Artists not members of the Society were
allowed to attend the sketching meetings on payment of a small fee per month. Two hours passed
pretty quietly, with great consumption of tobacco,
during the production of the sketches. At ten
o'clock these were collected by the attendant and
arranged on the long table, and were submitted
to the inspection and criticism of the members.
Very capital some of the sketches were. Doubt-

less the level of excellence is still maintained, and
may even be higher, but I am writing of thirty
or more years ago; and the quantity as well as
quality of work by some of the more facile sketchers

A LANGHAM FRIDAY NIGHT SKETCH.

was surprising. Some of the "Old Water Colour
Society" men attended these evenings, as Edward
Duncan, George Dodgson, and J. D. Watson, &c.
Charles Cattermole, the present secretary, Fitz-

gerald J. A. Pasquier, and Charles Keene were constant in their attendance. Arthur J. Lewis drew many a charcoal landscape, and Sir Francis Powell, Edwin Hayes, the two Greens, "C" Green and "T" Green, and F. Walker, then drawing on wood for journals and magazines, were familiar figures, with many others whose names do not recur to me. Among artists not members of the Society I have seen Calderon and J. E. Hodgson working at the subject of the evening.

On Fridays before the day of sending pictures to the principal exhibitions, soirees were held at Langham, when members and others contributed the works by which they hoped to be represented. Cards of invitation were issued for these evenings, to which amateurs and buyers gladly came. The picture-buyer was more frequently seen in those days, when he had not developed a coyness that now threatens to become habitual. There were fair chances of pictures being sold as well as seen, and many found purchasers.

When the pictures had been sufficiently studied, vocal and instrumental music enlivened the proceedings, but none of these gatherings was ever considered complete without the clever imitations of the popular actors and actresses of the day of Mr. J. A. Fitzgerald, the son of the Fitzgerald,

I believe, whom Byron mentions in his "English Bards and Scotch Reviewers."

About this time, my friend Clayton, although devoted to sculpture and painting, on academic lines, had acquired a knowledge of Gothic architecture under Salvin, for whom he had superintended the elaborate carved work in the choir of Wells Cathedral. At Wells, Clayton, who was facile of hand and omnivorous in his pursuit of art, became deeply impressed with the ancient glass in which the building is so rich.

His sketches of this glass were seen by R. C. Carpenter, the architect, who at once induced Clayton to design for him a window for a church then under his hands. From this incident, Clayton, a sculptor at heart, became a glass-painter, although for some time his work was divided between glass-painting, sculpture, and drawing on wood for the *Illustrated London News* and book-illustration. I have seen headings for songs by him, also a *Pilgrim's Progress* illustrated in outline, showing how impressed he was with the work of John Flaxman.

Walking with Smallfield one night from the Langham, he told me that Clayton wanted some assistance in figure-work, and suggested that I should offer my services. This I accordingly did, and was taken on for a few hours of an afternoon.

What I did was chiefly "squaring up" from Clayton's drawings. Sir, then Mr., Gilbert Scott was a friend of his, and gave to him all his glass-work and some of his sculpture. Clayton had a large commission from Sir Charles Nicholson, to whom he was introduced by his friend the late Thomas Woolner, for a long series of windows containing effigies of English worthies for the University buildings at Sydney, New South Wales. He was also engaged at this time on a similar commission for Sherborne Minster; with many of these large figures I helped. The cartoon paper was nailed to the wall of the workroom, and I mounted the household steps to get at and finish the upper parts.

Mr. Gilbert Scott had then in his office a pupil named Alfred Bell, who having served his time, turned his attention to designing for glass. This placed Mr. Scott in a delicate position. He was willing and anxious to serve both friend and pupil, yet did not see how he could distribute the large amount of glass-work daily coming in fairly and impartially without some bond of union existing between the two. He therefore suggested that they should go into partnership and work together. After much discussion pro and con, this was eventually carried out, and thus originated that collaboration of artists which, as Clayton & Bell,

has secured a European, if not a world-wide repu-
tation.

Under this new condition of affairs, my services
being no longer needed by my friend Clayton, he
gave me introductions to Messrs. Powell of White-
friars and to Mr. Lavers. I worked for both these
houses, more particularly the last, which found me
occasional employment for two or three years. I
have still by me a small account-book I kept of the
work I did for, and the payment I received from,
Mr. Lavers. Some of the entries are curious, reminding one of the accounts for the mystery plays
of the fourteenth and fifteenth centuries. Thus—

Aug. 1857.	Acts of Mercy, Hungry and Thirsty,	£4	0 0
Jan. 1858.	Altering four Prophets into Evan-		
	gelists, . . .	2	0 0

But I was destined to return to Clayton, or, as
we must now say, Clayton & Bell. I painted from
their designs and under their guidance a series of
circular medallions of angels with musical instruments for the ceiling of St. Michael's Church, Cornhill. It was on the scaffolding inside the church that
I first met my friend Richard Beavis, now of the Old
Water Colour Society, who was then employed as
their chief artist and designer by Messrs. Trollope.

In the early part of 1860, I was working for
Clayton & Bell, who had taken premises at Car-

dington Street, where they carried on the execution as well as designing of their work—taking a day or so each week to paint at home a small picture called the " Sexton's Sermon," the background of which, the interior of a belfry, had been carefully studied on the spot in the ancient church of Winchelsea. In April I went for them to Dublin on what turned out to be a wild-goose chase. Some client desired a Last Judgment or other subject designed with a curtain introduced similar to one that (as he wrote) was to be seen at St. Patrick's Cathedral. I got to Dublin, pleased to find that in crossing from Holyhead to Kingston I was free from the unpleasant effects I had experienced when crossing the Channel with Calderon on our way to Paris. It was late in the evening when I reached my destination. I put up at some Commercial Inn, and after supper and a pipe or two, smoked in company with the "travellers" staying there, turned in. Next morning, as early as I thought it would be convenient, I went armed with my letter of introduction to the Dean's house in Merrion Square.

I thought of another Dean of St. Patrick's as I went along, and hoped this one might not be like the gloomy genius I had read of in Scott and Thackeray. I was pleasantly disappointed. After waiting a short time, the Dean came into the room, an active, cheery old gentleman, with florid face and

E

white silky hair, who was the pink of courtesy.
He had never heard of or seen such a curtain—had
no remembrance of it whatever; "but we'll go and
see," said he, and, taking his hat and cane, kindly
accompanied me to the Cathedral. We searched
every niche and corner where any painting could
possibly be, without result. "Well," said the Dean,
"you'll have to paint him a curtain out of your
own head." So we parted. I wrote to Clayton
& Bell, and awaited further instructions. The next
day was Sunday. I went to Glasnevin Cemetery,
and saw the tomb and monument of "the great
Liberator." I was surprised at the number of
wretched mud-walled cabins (not worthy the name
of cottages) in the outskirts of the city, and much
amused at a funeral party, which seemed bent rather
on some festive merrymaking than going to spread
the grass quilt over a friend or relative. A long
string of jaunting-cars followed each other at a
hand-gallop; the pace was exhilarating by its speed,
and the merry jest seemed to be going round, for
the faces of the mourners had an expression of
joviality rather than of sorrow. On Monday I did
the Phœnix Park, the Zoological Gardens, Trinity
College, the Custom-House, and all the places and
sights of which a stranger is expected to do the
round, winding up the day with a performance at
the Queen's Theatre, of which I remember nothing

but that one of the actors, a very good comedian, one Webb by name, I recognised a year or two afterwards at the Marylebone Theatre, then, I think, under Mr. Warner's management, where he played Autolycus in "The Winter's Tale." He was one of the brothers Webb, who subsequently played the two Dromios in the "Comedy of Errors" at the Princess's.

Next morning I received my instructions, and returned to London with pleasant impressions of my brief stay in the Irish city, and of the genial kindness of the inhabitants with whom I came in contact.

OLD HOUSE, TARRING.

CHAPTER V

FREDERICK WALKER was a disciple of Leigh's, joining the school after I had left. I heard of him before we met as a very clever young fellow who drew by day at the British Museum and at Newman Street in the evening. He became a student of the Academy in 1858, but never advanced beyond the Antique School. It was not till the days of the Langham Society that I came to know him. Here he made few actual studies, but was ever making mental sketches, drawing with his eye, if not with his hand, and cultivating a naturally retentive memory, which enabled him to reproduce forms, lines, and expressions with ready certainty. On the Friday sketching evenings he shone with brilliance. His work, always excellent and replete with touches of nature, was

eagerly looked for at the hour when all the
sketches were gathered and shown together. Many

WALKER BEING INTRODUCED BY THACKERAY.
P. H. Calderon.

of these designs were the first thoughts of future
pictures. I possess one which is the primary idea
of a drawing he subsequently carried out—" The

Angler's Return,"—a boy showing the results
of his day's fishing to his mother and sister.
The boy opens his creel, tilted on one knee;
the good woman holds aloft a candle; the girl,
with hands clasped behind her, peers into the
basket, and a cat with straight up-lifted tail
asks for a savoury morsel of the spoil. One
of the fashions of the day is to decry a picture
that has a story as being "literary" or anecdotic,
but here is a story, as there are multitudes of
others, that can better be expressed by the
brush than by the pen. All the sketches made
by Walker on these evenings were good. I
never remember him producing a failure. An
amateur who devoted his days to commerce,
his nights to art at the Langham, told me that
Walker once offered him a batch of these sketches
at a very modest price, but he was unable to close
the bargain, which has been matter of regret to him
ever since. In those early days of Walker's career
we were very intimate; not a week passed without
his going to my house or I to his, when he lived
with his brothers and sisters near Baker Street. I
have seldom been without a nickname in my life.
Walker gave me two. Strolling about one evening,
we looked in at some humble sing-song place,
under the flimsy pretext of "studying character."
A lean hollow-cheeked, half-starved looking

creature began a song just as we entered, which for some reason took Walker's fancy. It was called

CARICATURE BY FREDERICK WALKER.

the " Lodging-House Cat," and described the voracious omnivorous appetite and destructive propensities of that fictitious animal. My memory

enables me to rescue from oblivion the chorus
only—

> " Rat-a-tat-tat, with its feet pit-a-pat,
> Beware of that monster—the lodging-house cat ! "

I was at once dubbed " the cat." But Walker
soon tired of this, and I became the " curly one,"

CARICATURE BY FREDERICK WALKER.

possibly in allusion to my hair, which was Hyperion-
like in those days. But Walker's nicknames grew
into disuse, and became forgotten ; the one that has
survived, and will cling as long as I live, is "Marco,"
which is more melodious in sound, and comes more
" trippingly on the tongue" than my harsh and ugly
surname.

Toothache in the Middle Ages
from the Original picture belonging to Mr. C.E. Mudie.

Walker had the keenest appreciation of humour, full of fun and friskiness, and ever ready to join in any " fetch " or " sell " short of that last infirmity of the idiot mind, a practical joke. At a fancy-dress ball given by Edwin Long, before that painter was elected A.R.A., Walker made a comical figure as Orson—a pocket-Hercules, clad in a bear-skin, and carrying a club of enormous proportions, but as harmless as it was hollow. At another, in a more serious mood, he appeared as Robespierre. The boots, knee-breeches, and short - waisted tightly fitting coat showed off his symmetrical figure to advantage ; for Walker, like many small people, was admirably proportioned, the people at his favourite Cookham always speaking of him as " the little model."

On the occasion of the celebration of the Tercentenary of Shakespeare, a few artists gave an entertainment at the Eyre Arm Assembly Rooms. G. D. Leslie's contribution to the amusement of the evening was a mock geological lecture, in which he enlarged on the surrounding district in its primeval state, and on the birds and beasts that then inhabited it. Walker drew one of these creatures from his imagination to illustrate the Bomphalor, a mammal that lived entirely by suction, in those days, when " the whole region for miles around the spot where I have the honour to

address you was one vast sea of mud; not mud in
the ordinary sense, as we degenerate creatures conceive it, but edible nutritious mud, the mighty
pabulum of the Phenactrite tribe!"

ANKLES, THE ATTENUATED VARIETY.

A ludicrous idea occurred to and was carried
out by Walker when he was once at Brighton with
my youngest brother, who, I may state here,
married F. W.'s twin-sister. The day was warm,

with no wind to speak of—the sea, like glass.
The pair (F. W. and my brother) entered a bathing-
machine, which was drawn a little distance from
shore as usual.   A few minutes, and a most *un*usual
sight was presented to the people on the beach.

ANKLES, THE BULBOUS TYPE.

In the gleaming water two black objects appeared.
All but motionless at first, they at length began
to move—to bob up and down.   Opera-glasses and
telescopes were brought to bear on these strange
creatures of the deep, when it was found that

each was a human head surmounted by *a tall
hat!* A hand would now and then appear above
the water holding a walking-cane. To read this
scarcely excites a smile, but imagine the scene,

A PROUD MOTHER.

and one can understand what loud laughter and
shouts came from the shore.

I have referred to the trip taken to the South
of France in company with Calderon in the chapter
on Birds, and how we came back earlier than we

at first intended. This incident supplied a motive
for a "fetch" in which Walker took part. At
the time of which I write, Calderon and I lived
but a few doors apart, in Hill Road, St. John's
Wood. He had a nearly full-sized billiard-table,
on which we played many a game together.
We were thus engaged one evening after our
return when the game was interrupted by loud
ringing of the "door-bells," both "visitors'" and
"servants'." Much annoyance had been experienced during the past few nights by "runaway
rings." On hearing the noise made by these
dreadful bells, we rushed upstairs, cues in hand,
to see if we could catch the culprits. To our
surprise, on opening the street door, we found a
group of men assembled on the top step under
the house-porch carrying lighted Japanese lanterns.
These were Walker, Leslie, Hodgson, and the rest
of the clique, who had come as a deputation to
welcome our return to the mother country. Walker
bore a scroll which looked like an address, Leslie
a circular disc of deal covered with tin-foil, to
which a blue ribbon was attached, to represent an
enormous silver medal. We went into the house.
The medal, on which Walker had painted a profile
caricature of me, was presented, and pinned to
my breast; the supposed address being unrolled,
displayed a cartoon of a poodle-dog and a cat,

both having human heads, running their hardest
from the South of France. A Frenchman in an
attitude of astonishment, standing by a sign-post
marked "Boulogne," showed that the pair were
well on their way home. The poodle was Calderon,
with a tin saucepan tied to his tail labelled
"Hampden," a picture he had begun that year;
the "cat," with eye-glass flying in the wind, was of
course the writer. The remainder of the evening
was merrily spent, with pipes, cigarettes, and the
social glass, or "mallet," as whisky-and-water was
known among the clique. This term originated
from a visit Walker and I paid to a hostelry close
by Langham Chambers, in the bar of which was
hung a painting of a dead dog with the following
inscription in gold letters underneath :—

> "Poor Trust is dead and cold, you see;
>   Bad pay the deed has done.
> No mallet you'll expect of me;
>   'Tis up with that 'ere fun."

Walker is known most widely by his woodcuts
in *Once a Week*, *The Cornhill Magazine*, *Good
Words*, *Sunday at Home*, &c. Influenced in some
measure by the drawing of Menzel and the
Tennyson illustrations by the Pre-Raphaelites, he
eventually formed a style of his own. He may
be said to have founded, or to have assisted in

founding, that modern school of illustration which is the most remarkable development of British art in the latter half of this century. Pinwell, Small, Fildes, Herkomer, and others were influenced by him : the latter to this day calls him affectionately " master."

In the intervals of his wood-drawing, Walker was teaching himself to colour both in oils and water. His first oil picture, " The Lost Path " (1863), a poor woman in a snowstorm clasping a child to her breast, was sent to the Academy and hung high. He did not send again until 1867, when he exhibited " The Bathers." This also was unfavourably hung ; but he persevered, and sent annually one picture to the Academy as long as he lived. Mr. William Agnew bought " The Bathers," though it was not then a popular picture, and remained for many years on his hands, I believe. Each succeeding picture, with the exception of " At the Bar " and " The Right of Way," passed through the same hands. Some years before Walker was elected Associate of the Academy (1871), he made a most successful début as Associate of the Society of Painters in Water Colours in 1864. In the Summer Exhibition of that year he had " Spring "—a young girl gathering primroses in a wood—and " Philip in Church," which in 1867 gained a second-class medal at the

Paris International, the only English drawing that gained that distinction.

I have heard that the late Mr. Topham, member of the Society, and a very intimate friend of Mr. William Agnew, wrote to that gentleman in high praise of Walker's "Spring," of which he had had ample opportunities of judging as one of the arrangers of the Exhibition. He went so far as to say that this young artist combined the excellences of W. Hunt and Mulready, and superadded original qualities of his own. The price of the drawing, he added, was very high for so young a man. Mr. Agnew wrote to say he would be at the private view at an early hour. That day came, and so did Mr. Agnew according to promise. Topham was ready to receive him, and showed him the drawing. Mr. Agnew saw, approved, and signified his desire to become its possessor at the price named.

Meanwhile a young man in a highly wrought state of excitement had been nervously biting his nails, as he restlessly stood near the entrance door of the gallery. Topham went over to him, brought him up, and introduced him to Agnew as Fred Walker. They shook hands. The great picture merchant spoke in high terms of the drawing, and said he would be glad to have it. The pleasure and excitement overcame poor Walker—his heart was too full for speech. He burst into tears, and gasping out, "I must go and tell my mother!" rushed from the place. Topham ran after him, bidding him to be sure to come back to lunch. Back he came in due time, calm, self-possessed, and beaming with content. Over the sherry and biscuits a friendship was established between painter and dealer which was never interrupted, and lasted to the end of a life all too short for friendship, though not for fame.

Some years after, Walker went to Algiers for the sake of his health, but the climate did not suit him; he became restless, home-sick, and despondent. George Leslie in "Our River" tells how Miss Jekyll was staying there with some friends, and when about to leave for England, invited him to accompany them. His one wish was to be again in London and riding in a hansom cab. Poor fellow! he was weak and broken down. Miss Jekyll looked after him with the tenderness of a sister, and arriving at Charing Cross, said, "There, Mr. Walker, you are once more in London, and there is a hansom cab." On a fishing excursion in Scotland with his friend Mr. Theodore Watts, he caught cold, had violent inflammation of the lungs, and his friends were shocked by hearing of his death, in many instances before they had realised that he was dangerously ill.

I have attended many funerals in my time. I was present at that of John Leech, and saw Charles Dickens shake hands with Mark Lemon over the grave of Clarkson Stanfield. For Sir Edwin Landseer's funeral the members met in the Assembly Room of the old Academy in Trafalgar Square; each had a voluminous silk band arranged on his hat, and a long cloak, scanty of folds, tied on his shoulders. These fashions have happily died out. Walker, Poynter, Vicat Cole and I rode in the same coach from the Academy to St. Paul's Cathedral. Along the route many of the shops were closed out of respect for the great animal-painter, so popular had he been with all classes. One touch of (horse or dog) nature makes all Britons kin. The service was dignified and impressive. When all was over, Walker, Cole, Poynter, and myself returned in the same coach. Little did I then think that in less than two years I should be a mourner at a service of simpler, and to me far sadder kind.

It was early in June 1875 that a small band of friends went by train from Paddington one morning, to attend the funeral of F. Walker. My brother, J. G. Marks, rode down with the body the night before from St. Petersburgh Place to Cookham in a covered van. It was placed in an adjoining cottage, to be carried thence to the grave. Agnew, Clayton, Leslie, Prinsep, Storey, Hodgson were among those who knelt or stood around it as the concluding prayers were read. To say there was not a dry eye among the mourners is to give no idea of the grief felt by them. Audible sobs came from the breasts of most. The poor lad could not have been laid in the earth under conditions and in a scene more appropriate to his art, or in greater harmony with his feeling for nature. The sheep browsed around the neighbouring graves, the village children, who knew him in life, looked on hushed and subdued into something like awe. Beyond all was the river sparkling in the sunshine, the river he loved so well, flowing swiftly and silently by.

The melancholy morning of this day was succeeded by an afternoon almost equally sad. William Agnew, my brother John, and I went to Petersburgh Place to look over the works Walker had left, with a view to their ultimate sale at Christie's. The studio in the garden was hushed and silent as the grave ; the carpet had been taken up, portfolios, easels, and other properties tidily arranged, and a stack of canvases, faces inwards, stood against the wall. One considerably larger than the others we knew must be "At the Bar," the first picture exhibited after Walker had attained his A.R.A., unique among his works for its depth of tragic expression. From the first it had been an unfortunate picture.

Hung in a corner of the lecture-room, it was looked on coldly by his confreres on the varnishing-days, and few, if any, had a word of compliment or congratulation.   Private-view day arrived and ended without the picture being sold.   W. Agnew could not see his way to become the purchaser—size and subject were against its saleability.   It was emphatically a "gallery picture," very low in tone, the only light being the face of the prisoner at the bar, with so terrible an expression, like that of some hunted wild animal brought to bay—it haunted one's memory, and was scarcely a subject to appeal to the average picture-buyer.   On turning the picture round to the light, we found that poor Walker had, in a fit of anger and mortification, obliterated the head, not by merely painting it out, but by rubbing it with pumice-stone to the actual canvas, till only a few dark blurred spots were left to show where the shadows of the brow and mouth had been.   With the inspection of this work our mournful task came to an end, and we came away.

The picture was kept for many years by the executors, who were irresolute in coming to any conclusion as to what should be done with it.   They at length persuaded R. W. Macbeth, A.R.A., whose admirable etchings from Walker's works are known to every one, to repaint the head, which he did (partly aided by a little oil replica exhibited in the

Dudley in 1872), and "At the Bar" was sent to
Christie's, and sold for a sum considerably under
100 guineas.

We, that is, my wife, self, and family, passed
the month of August 1863 at Swanage, on the
Dorset coast. After a while we were joined by
Calderon and his wife, and by Fred Walker and
his sister Fanny. The Calderons, who stayed but
a few days, put up at the hotel. The Walkers
found lodgings in the High Street, where self and
family were already located, over the shop of a
greengrocer, by name Herlock. The general
aspect of the street is well rendered in the sketch,
and the positions of our respective lodgings, from
the windows of which Walker and I are looking
with wonder, not unmixed with awe, at the number
of "game legs" presented to our view. There are
extensive stone quarries in the immediate neighbourhood, and the working of these, at the time
of which I write, at least, seemed to be accompanied with serious detriment to the limbs, if not
to the lives, of the operatives. I happened, shortly
after Walker's arrival, to make the exaggerated
statement that every other man one met had one

leg maimed or missing: this remark may have
suggested the sketch.   The action of the boat-
man with the wooden leg is admirable as he
stumps down hill; note also the sly touch of
another wooden-legged man · behind him calling at

MARKS'S LANDLORD —
the Great Herlock.

the bootmaker's. Our landlord, Herlock, Walker
immortalised in another sketch; an active, wiry,
hatchet-faced little man, with the full complement
of limbs.   His usual salutation when I came down
before breakfast was "Maarnin, Zur—a smart

maarnin' for the mush-a-roons, Zur." I have sometimes wondered if Walker thought of his picture the
"Mushroom Gatherers" while staying at Swanage
—a picture he never finished, and which, it is pleasant to know, is owned by one of his fast friends

"so early in the morning"

and admirers, George Leslie. I can fancy him
thinking it out in the early dawn as he sat huddled
in his bedroom window-seat, wrapped in a blanket,
looking out on the vast downs, which appeared
vaster still by the doubtful light of "so early in the
morning."

In the sketch called "Genius, &c.," Calderon and I are portrayed blowing tobacco smoke into an ants' nest while resting during a breezy walk on a Sunday morning on the sea-girt cliffs. The shadow of F. W. thrown on the crisp and chalky turf indicates his sense of horror at our proceedings. One week-day morning donkeys were hired and ridden by Mrs. Calderon and Miss Walker, while the rest of the party tramped on foot. Calderon is depicted endeavouring to persuade one of the animals to mend his pace, not by any of the brutal methods peculiar to professional donkeyboys, but by gentle pressure and laying on of hands. During our stay, F. W. and I made the acquaintance of a good-natured genial farmer named Hunt, who lived in a quaint old-fashioned stone-built house some little distance from the town. The first time we went to his place he showed us over the farm, its belongings and buildings, the garden and the orchard. While doing the latter he would discourse learnedly on different varieties of apple, presenting Walker at every period of his lecture with a cucumber or a vegetable marrow. In short, he so loaded the young painter with produce of one kind or another, that he looked like a walking Covent Garden in miniature, and had much ado to carry all his gifts at once. I felt bound to introduce this sketch, as without it

The Donkey Boys

SWANAGE—THE DONKEY RIDE.

The Visit to the Orchard.

SWANAGE.

the record of the pleasant days spent at Swanage
would be incomplete.

The most elaborate pen-and-ink Walker drawing

'Genius - under the influence
of fresh air and beautiful
scenery. — Sunday Aug 30.1863

I have is that which shows him wandering alone
on the cliffs at Torquay, where he suddenly sees
as in a vision his friends of the St. John's Wood

Clique, which is here reproduced as a plate. The original bears the date "Torquay Asylum, 1865." It became mine in this wise. The members of the Clique at one time had sketching meetings at each other's houses. One evening all of us were at Walker's; in the course of it he produced the drawing. Loud were we in its praise, and each secretly hoped that he might become its owner. It would have been invidious to have singled out an individual. Walker felt the difficulty, and, after some discussion, it was decided to draw lots for the sketch. This was done straightway; the fortunate lot fell to my share, and the sketch became mine. I may mention in passing, that this was the only object I ever won in a raffle in my life, and for that reason, if for no other, was not likely to forget the fact. To describe the design—the principal figure is extremely like F. W. in face and build. Prominent in the ghostly group are Calderon and myself, arm in arm. We were accustomed to give Calderon the nickname of "the fiend," a circumstance hinted at by the budding horns on the forehead. I, "the all-licensed jester," carry a fool's bauble in one hand, the single eyeglass which I wore for many years in the other. Behind these is a very elongated and attenuated George Leslie, bearing a diminutive George Storey, who

The Jesters Text.
The subject of this years discourse, beloved brethren, is taken from the Book of Proverbs. *. (Vide Royal Academy Catalogue for 1864.)

J. E. HODGSON

A SERMON TO THE CLIQUE.

is comparatively short of stature. These are habited
in theatrical shepherds' costumes which they once
wore at a fancy-dress ball. Hodgson, perhaps
the least successful figure of the composition, in
an Elizabethan dress, reclines beyond. In front
we see D. W. Wynfield with a genealogical tree,
for he was great on family histories, and an
authority on heraldry and armorial bearings, accompanied by Yeames gleefully displaying a wedding-
ring, an allusion to his marriage, which took place
that year. Two of the figures bear the gridiron
badge on their breasts. The serpent and the file
refer to a sermon which I preached for many
years and in many places from the well-known
text, "They shall gnaw a file and flee into the
mountains of Hepsidam."

CHAPTER VI

FREDERICK WALKER AND RUSKIN

IN little more than six weeks after Walker's death, his remaining works, his easels, cabinets, and studio properties, were sold by Messrs. Christie, Manson, & Wood on July 17, 1875. There were 142 lots in all, consisting chiefly of pencil and sepia drawings, water-colour sketches, with studies and a few unfinished pictures in oil and water. The sale realised the satisfactory sum (considering the small number of items) of over £3000. Before the sale a meeting was held at the Arts Club, at which it was resolved that all who felt affection for the man or sympathy with his work should be invited to contribute to a Walker memorial fund. A large and influential committee, including some of the brightest names in British art, was at once formed, which decided to hold an exhibition of Walker's work. From these an executive committee was chosen, who at once went energetically to work. Owners of pictures or drawings were at once communicated with, and all without exception responded generously to the appeals for loans. Mr. Deschamps kindly gave the free use of his gallery for the purpose of the exhibition, which was opened to the public early in January 1876 with 150 examples of Walker's art.

The exhibition having been finally arranged, it was thought that, as I had some slight acquaintance with Mr. Ruskin, it would be well to write to him, and ask him to give his opinion of the exhibition, as a means of drawing a larger share of public attention to it. This I accordingly did; it led to the appearance of Mr. Ruskin's memorable letter which appeared in the *Times* newspaper.

"January 7, 1876.

" DEAR MR. RUSKIN,—I venture to ask you, on the strength of our former acquaintance, if you would do an act of kindness in the cause of art. You have probably heard that there is to be an exhibition of the late F. Walker's works at Deschamps' gallery, 168 New Bond Street. It is a means both of making these same works more widely known to the public, and of adding to the fund which has been subscribed for his sister. It has occurred to me that, if you would go to the exhibition (it opens on Tuesday next), and record, say, in a letter to the *Times*, some of your impressions and opinions about Walker's work, you would be greatly helping the cause we have in hand. A word from one who has done so much

for art as you have done would have great weight ;
and I venture to hope that, notwithstanding your late
public announcement that you are very 'cross and
ill-natured,' you will be able to see your way to
accede to my request.

"I may mention that I don't write officially as
Hon. Sec. of the committee, but as a friend of
Walker and an admirer of yours.—Believe me,
faithfully yours,   H. S. M."

Mr. Ruskin wrote the desired letter at once, and
sent it by Arthur Severn to me. It was on a Sunday
afternoon we read it together, and were both somewhat depressed by its general tone. I sent it on to
the *Times* office, and wrote to Mr. Ruskin acknow-
ledging its receipt, and ventured to murmur gently
at his criticism. This letter and his characteristic
reply, though previous in date, will fall better in
their place after the perusal of the celebrated
Times letter.

From the "Times," Thursday, January 20, 1876.

THE FREDERICK WALKER EXHIBITION.

Mr. H. Stacy Marks, A.R.A., the honorary secretary to the "Walker Memorial Fund," has received
the following letter from Mr. Ruskin, in answer
to a request that Mr. Ruskin would record in

some way his impression of the late Mr. Frederick
Walker's works :—

   " DEAR MR. MARKS,—You ask me to say what I
feel of Frederick Walker's work, now seen in some
collective mass, as far as anything can be seen in
black-veiled London.   You have long known my
admiration of his genius, my delight in many
passages of his art.   These, while he lived, were
all I cared to express.   If you will have me speak
of him now, I must speak the whole truth of what
I feel, namely, that every soul in London interested
in art ought to go to see that exhibition, and, amid
all the beauty and the sadness of it, very diligently
to try and examine themselves as to the share they
have had, in their own busy modern life, in arresting
the power of this man at the point where it stayed.
Very chief share they have had assuredly.   But
he himself, in the liberal and radical temper of
modern youth, has had his own part in casting
down his strength, following wantonly or obstinately
his own fancies wherever they led him.   For instance, it being Nature's opinion that sky should
usually be blue, and it being Mr. Walker's opinion
that it should be the colour of buff plaster, he
resolutely makes it so, for his own isolated satisfaction, partly in affectation also, buff skies being
considered by the public more sentimental than blue

ones.   Again, the laws of all good painting having
been long ago determined by absolute masters,
whose work cannot be bettered or departed from ;
Titian having determined for ever what oil-paint-
ing is, Angelico what tempera-painting is, Perugino
what fresco-painting is, two hundred years of noble
miniature-painting what minutest work on ivory is,
and in modern times a score of entirely skilful and
disciplined draughtsmen what pure water-colour and
pure body-colour painting on paper are (Turner's
Yorkshire drawing of Hornby Castle, now at
Kensington, and John Lewis's ' Encampment under
Sinai,' being namable at once as unsurpassable
standards) ; here is Mr. Walker refusing to learn
anything from any of those schools or masters, but
inventing a semi-miniature, quarter fresco, quarter
wash manner of his own, exquisitely clever, and
reaching, under such clever management, delightfullest results here and there, but which betrays
his genius into perpetual experiment instead of
achievement, and his life into woful vacillation
between the good, old, quiet room of the Water
Colour Society, and your labyrinthine magnificence
at Burlington House.

" Lastly, and in worst error, the libraries of
England being full of true and noble books, her
annals of true and noble history, and her traditions
of beautiful and noble, in these scientific times I

must say, I suppose mythology—not religious—from all these elements of mental education and subjects of serviceable art, he turns recklessly away to enrich the advertisements of the circulating library—to sketch whatever pleases his fancy, barefooted, or in dainty boots of modern beggary and fashion, and enforce with laboriously symbolical pathos his adherence to Justice Shallow's sublime theology that 'all shall die.'

"That theology has indeed been preached by stronger men again and again, from Horace's days to our own, but never to so little purpose. 'Let us eat and drink, for to-morrow we die,' said wisely, in his way, the Latin farmer, who ate his beans and bacon in comfort, had his suppers of the gods on the fair earth, with his servants jesting round the table, and left eternal monuments of earthly wisdom and of cricket-song. 'Let us labour and be just, for to-morrow we die, and after death the judgment,' said Holbein and Dürer, and left eternal monuments of upright human toil and honourable gloom of godly fear. 'Let us rejoice and be exceeding glad, for to-morrow we die and shall be with God,' said Angelico and Giotto, and left eternal monuments of divinely blazoned heraldry of heaven. 'Let us smoke pipes, make money, read bad novels, walk in bad air, and say sentimentally how sick we are in the afternoon, for to-morrow we die and shall be made ourselves clay pipes,' says the modern world, and drags this poor bright painter down into the abyss with it, vainly clutching at a handful of scent and flowers in the May gardens.

"Under which sorrowful terms, being told also by your grand Academicians that he should paint the nude, and accordingly wasting a year or two of his life in trying to paint schoolboys' backs and legs without their shirts or breeches, and with such other magazine material as he can pick up of sick gipsies, faded gentlewomen, pretty girls disguised as hawkers, and the red-roofed or grey remnants of old English villages and manor-houses, last wrecks of the country's peace and honour, remaining yet visible among the black ravages of its ruin, he supplies the demands of his temporary public, scarcely patient, even now that he is gone, to pause beside his delicate tulips or under his sharp-leaved willows, and repent for the passing tints and falling petals of the life that might have been so precious, and perhaps, in better days, prolonged.

"That is the main moral of the exhibition. Of the beauty of the drawings, accepting them for what they aim at being, there is little need that I should add anything to what has been said rightly by the chief organs of the London press. Nothing can go beyond them in subtlety of exhibited touch (to be distinguished, however, observe always, from the serene completion of master's work, disdaining the applause to be gained by its manifestation) ; their harmonies of amber-colour and purple are full of exquisite beauty in their chosen key ; their composition always graceful, often admirable, and the sympathy they express with all conditions of human life most kind and true : not without power of rendering character, which would have been more recognised in an inferior artist, because it would have been less restrained by the love of beauty.

"I might, perhaps, in my days of youth and good fortune, have written what the public would have called 'eloquent passages' on the subjects of the 'Almshouse' and the 'Old Gate ;' being now myself old and decrepit (besides being much bothered with beggars, and in perpetual feud with parish officers), and having seen every building I cared for in the world ruined, I pass these two pictures somewhat hastily by, and try to enjoy myself a little in the cottage-gardens. Only one of them, however—No. 71—has right sunshine in it, and that is a sort of walled paddock, where I begin directly to feel uncomfortable about the lamb, lest perchance some front shop in the cottages belong to a butcher. If only it and I could get away to a bit of thymy hillside, we should be so much happier, leaving the luminous—perhaps too ideally luminous — child to adorn the pathetic paddock.   I am too shy to speak to either of those beautiful ladies among the lilies (37, 67), and take refuge among the shy children before the 'Chaplain's Daughter' (20)—delightfullest, it seems to me, of the minor designs, and a piece of most true and wise satire.   The sketches of the 'Daughter of Heth' go far to tempt me to read the novel, and, ashamed of this weakness, I retreat resolutely to the side of the exemplary young girl knitting in the 'Old Farm Garden' (33), and would pick up the ball of worsted for her, but that I wouldn't for the world disappoint the cat.   No drawing in the room is more delicately completed than this unpretending subject, and the flower painting in it, for instantaneous grace of creative touch, cannot be rivalled; it is worth all the Dutch flower-pieces in the world.

"Much instructed, and more humiliated, by passage after passage of its rapidly-grouped colour, I get finally away into the comfortable corner beside the salmon-fisher and the mushrooms; and the last-named drawing—despise me who may—keeps me till I've no more time to stay, for it entirely beats my dear old William Hunt in the simplicity of its execution, and rivals him in the subtlest truth.

"I say nothing of the 'Fishmonger's Stall' (62), though there are qualities of the same kind in these also, for they somewhat provoke me by their waste of time; the labour spent on one of them would have painted twenty instructive studies of fish of their real size. And it is well for artists in general to observe that when they do condescend to paint still life carefully, whether fruit, fungi, or fish, it must at least be of the real size. The portrait of a man or woman is only justifiably made small that it may be portable, but nobody wants to carry about the miniature of a cod; and if the reader will waste five minutes of his season in London in the National Gallery, he may see in the hand of Perugino's Tobias a fish worth all these on the boards together.

"Some blame of the same kind attaches to the marvellous drawing No. 68. It is all very well for a young artist to show how much work he can put into an inch, but very painful for an old gentleman of fifty-seven to have to make out all the groups through a magnifying-glass. I could say something malicious about the boat, in consequence of the effect of this exertion on my temper, but will not, and leave with unqualified praise the remainder of the lesser drawings to the attention which each will variously reward.

"Nor, in what I have already, it may be thought,

too bluntly said, ought the friends of the noble artist to feel that I am unkind. It is because I know his real power more deeply than any of the admirers who give him indiscriminate applause, that I think it right distinctly to mark the causes which prevented his reaching heights they did not conceive, and ended by placing one more tablet in the street of tombs, which the passionate folly and uninstructed confusion of modern English society prolong with dark perspective above the graves of its youth.

"I am, dear Marks, always very faithfully yours,

"J. RUSKIN."

Here are the two letters referred to previously :—

"15 HAMILTON TERRACE, N.W.,
January 18, 1876.

"MY DEAR MR. RUSKIN,—I sent your manuscript to the *Times* early this morning, so perhaps we may see it in print to-morrow.

"If I also may speak 'the whole truth,' I would say that I read your notes with a feeling of disappointment. I had hoped that he who praised Frère so highly, finding in him 'the grace of Reynolds and the purity of Angelico' (I quote from memory), and who told us that 'if we are now to do anything great, good, or religious, it must be got out of our own little island, railroads and all,'—I had hoped, I say, that he who told us this would have found more to admire in the works of one so essentially English, and who has given us so many pure and exquisite renderings of childhood and womanhood. It may be that my friendship for the man has led me to over-rate the painter, but I have been in company with his collected works some days while assisting to hang them, and they grew upon me hourly, impressing more forcibly than ever the opinion I had long entertained that Walker was one of our greatest artists.

"And now, having said my say, I hope you will believe that I write this, not angrily, but sadly ; and though I would have wished you could praise Walker more, I am not the less grateful to you for what you have said, and for the kind promptitude with which you have said it.—Believe me to be very faithfully yours,   H. S. M."

"HERNE HILL,
19th January 1876.

"DEAR MR. MARKS,—I am grateful to you for sending the letter as it stood, and trust that it may be as useful, in practical recommendation of the exhibition, as if it had been all friendly or laudatory. I do not wonder it disappointed you—it disappointed me—for I never know what is in my head, now, till I look for it. But do not think it argues change of temper since I wrote the Frère review, or a wanton praise of one man and blame of another. Every syllable of my criticism, these last twenty years, is weighed like apothecaries' drugs, whether it be prussic acid (which I can't ever distil to the bitterness I want), or perfumery of the Rimmel-smoothest. You all of you think I know nothing of my trade ; pick out what you like, and say, 'Well, for Ruskin, that's not so bad,' and 'What a fool that fellow is!' when it's what you don't agree with—and of course, that way, you never really understand a word I say.

"I wrote of Frère, first, he had the 'simplicity of Wordsworth.' Well, he lived in a village, loved it, and painted what he saw there. (Hook has done something of the kind, though not so faithfully, for Clovelly.) But you don't suppose there's any 'simplicity' in Walker! All those peasants of his are got up for the stage. Look at the flutter of that girl's apron under the apple-tree ; look at the ridi-culous mower, galvanised-Elgin in his attitude (and the sweep of the scythe utterly out of draw-ing, by the way). You don't suppose that flock of geese is done simply? It is elaborately affected—straining to express the feelings of a cockney who had never before seen a goose in his life, web-footed. You don't suppose those children in the

'Chaplain's Daughter' are simple? They are as artificial as the Sistine Chapel, and *yet* he can't be content with them, but must put in his little fashionable wretch, to mix another flavour with them—and that a nasty one.

"Again, I said of Frère, 'He has the grace of Reynolds.' At the time I wrote (he has much declined since) the masterful facility and serenity of Frère's broad touch were no less inimitable than Reynolds' was. Walker's, with all its skill, is an agony of labour. Look at the rose in the breast of Circe in the Old Masters; it is worth all Walker's flower-beds in a row; and that was Frère's method of work when I wrote that review.

"Lastly, I said he had 'the holiness of Angelico.' The picture I was speaking of, 'The Prayer,' is an entirely immortal work in representing the sacredest moment in the day of a peasant mother and child. But there is no evidence in the entire Walker exhibition that he ever had heard of such a thing as prayer. He seems to be one of your modern clique of Sons of Heth, who don't even know the religion of the Hittites.

"And lastly, you all of you fancy, I suppose, that I write heartlessly, and don't consider how dear and good and pleasant people were. But what business have you to mix up your hearts and brains in a mess? It is not because my affections are weak, but because they are much too strong to be mistaken for anything else, that I can keep clear of them—when their conversation is not wanted.

"And I must not close my letter without asking you to believe that it is owing to what I know of your own kindness of heart that I take these pains to justify myself to you for what I have written; for although for the moment it may give you more pain that I should thus further insist on the failings of your friend's work, I trust you will ultimately have more contentment in knowing that I cared for you both, and wrote with extreme earnestness and deliberation, than in remaining under any impression of having merely drawn me into an ebullition of momentary ill-temper. And I trust that you will kindly accept the expression of my friendly feeling to yourself, and continue to think of me as faithfully yours, J. RUSKIN.

"H. STACY MARKS, Esq."

"15 HAMILTON TERRACE, N.W.,
January 22, 1876.

"MY DEAR MR. RUSKIN,—I am very glad the *Times* inserted your letter, as I asked the editor to do, at full length.

"It cannot fail to draw many visitors to the Walker

Exhibition, even were it less laudatory than it is. In fact, I heard of people being in the gallery on Thursday afternoon with the letter cut from the paper, and alternately studying the words and the pictures.

"I feel that I cannot argue the question of Walker's merit with a critic so subtle as yourself, and though agreeing with you in many points, especially many in your last letter to me (for I went down and had another look after receiving it), I would rather not, even if I could, pursue the subject further.

"I must, however, reply to one or two remarks in your last. I, for one, have always given you credit for the utmost sincerity and deliberation in your judgments on art, and have always honestly tried not to misunderstand you. After this, you will, I hope, except me from those—if any such there are—who think that you write 'heartlessly;' and I need hardly say that I accept and reciprocate with heartfelt pleasure the sentiments of goodwill that you express towards me. I thank you most warmly both for your public and your private ones, and our correspondence, which I shall carefully preserve, will always afford me a very pleasant reminiscence.—Believe me to be faithfully yours,

"H. S. M."

Here our correspondence ended for the present. I became more intimate with Mr. Ruskin later, and received several letters from him, samples of which will be given in another chapter.

CHAPTER VII

CHARLES KEENE

I FORGET in what year I made the acquaintance of Charles Keene, but it must have been in the late fifties, when he was sending an occasional drawing to *Punch*.

GRAVESEND.

I was much struck with his quaint and characteristic appearance, not unlike one of those cavaliers he would often draw, in the days of Langham Chambers, on the Friday evenings of the Sketching Club. Many of these drawings revealed the more

romantic and imaginative side of Keene's nature,
of which those who know him only by his work for
Punch have little or no idea.

In conversation he was amiable, gravely genial,
and had much acquaintance with old world lore.
We soon got to like each other; the liking developed into friendship, that lasted more than thirty
years, and ended only with his death.

A very enjoyable time I had in these early days
with Charles Keene. The Gravesend watermen
owned at that time a fleet of very fast-sailing vessels
of small size, which supplied Billingsgate market
with fish. They were called hatch-boats, from the
long hatch or hatchway running fore and aft up the
centre of the vessel, so constructed as to offer great
facility for taking in and discharging fish. One of
these Keene chartered for a few days, the "William
and Mary of Gravesend," and we embarked for a
little cruise in the mouths of the Thames and
Medway, one fine forenoon early in August. We
took provisions, a large piece of boiled salt beef, a
sack of potatoes, eggs, and butter, &c. The crew
consisted of two men, and all preparations having
been made, we set sail. The sleeping accom-
modation consisted of two bunks for passengers in
the bows, and a confined hole called by courtesy
the fo'ksle beyond, in which the crew slept. We
retired early. Accustomed to curl myself up when

going to sleep, I bewailed the extreme narrowness of

AT THE MOUTH OF THE THAMES WITH CHARLES KEENE.

my bunk, when C. K. at once stopped my objections

by exclaiming with Maria in "Twelfth Night," "I
have wit enough to lie straight in my bed!" We
soon dropped off to sleep, the gruff talk of the
crew on the eternal subject of boats and fishing
being the last recognisable sound.   Keene was
accustomed at that time to draw straight from any

ON THE "WILLIAM AND MARY" OFF QUEENBOROUGH.

object in pen and ink, without preparatory pencilling, as a means of obtaining certainty and sure-
ness of hand. Wishing to emulate his example, I
began to do likewise. Each of us wore an ink-bottle
suspended from our waistcoat buttons, and carried oblong sketch-books. But for our Bohemian

appearance we might have been taken for tax-gatherers. We drew each other, the boatmen, parts of the vessel, occasionally going ashore for a bit of landscape. C. K. was cook, made the coffee and boiled the eggs for breakfast, and the potatoes in their jackets for dinner. One day we went ashore at Gillingham, and having sketched some time, lunched at the "Ship Inn," for we were a little tired of continual salt junk. There was nothing to be had but pork chops, which Keene did not care for, and managed but about half a one. By that time I had demolished the remainder, and feeling that the inn people might feel their cooking had been slighted, when they beheld what scant justice had been done to it by one of us, I coolly divided the picked bones into equal shares and placed one lot on Keene's plate. He was not angry, only saying with his sad smile, "You are a fellow!" This "You are a fellow" was an exclamation of surprise or mild reproof often used by Keene. In the earlier days of our friendship he asked me "if I smoked dottles?" "No!" "You are a fellow!" For the sake of the uninitiated who don't know what "dottles" are, it may be explained that when a pipe is smoked out there is a portion left at the bottom of the bowl, dark and damp from the nicotine which has drained through the tobacco already consumed.

Keene would collect and dry these carefully, and eventually smoke them with much zest. They would turn an ordinary smoker sick, so rank and strong are they, and impart an odour which the old novels used to say may be "more easily imagined than described!" A story goes to the effect that Keene once attended a wedding after a pipe or two of "dottles." There was a fragrance about the church that day, but it was not of incense or of flowers.

But to resume. The egg-shells from breakfast were saved and started, with lighted candle-ends in them as ballast, after dusk on the stream, and on a calm night would float a considerable distance down the tide before becoming extinguished. Once the coast-guard's boat came alongside, and the officer wanted to know what we were doing. This circumstance tickled Keene immensely, and he exploded in gentle chuckles for some time afterwards. But neither this nor any other freak could raise a smile upon the faces of our crew. I never knew such stolid, impassive creatures, or more impervious to fun of any kind. I laid myself out to make them laugh, but though I indulged in the most frivolous and ridiculous antics I could invent, never succeeded in making them smile.

It was about sixteen years after this before I again went out with Keene. He had recommended Southwold in Suffolk as a good sketching ground, and, in company with Edward Edwards and J. E. Rogers, we took train to Darsham and thence by coach to Southwold. I liked the place much, and in the following July took the family down, and we stayed there some weeks. South-wold and the adjoining picturesque village of Walberswick, on the opposite bank of the river

BENFLEET.

Blythe, were then comparatively unknown to artists, and white umbrellas were few in the land. A picture by Hamilton Maccallum, irreverently entitled "Wobbleswick Ferry," appeared in the Academy in 1875, and this was, I think, the first, or all but the first, painted in the neighbourhood. The old ferryman was a character. When he was asked, " Well, Todd, what do you think of the weather?" he was careful not to commit himself by rash prophecies, and would answer, " Well, I don't know, sir; it might be eggs, and it might be young 'uns."

Though a drinker of beer, he did not believe in spirits, and likened a dram to "a flash of lightning in a gooseberry bush." " There ain't no good in it; it's no sooner in yer than it's out of yer!" Some years later Edwards took a house at Dunwich, which has suffered so much from the encroachments of the sea that very little of the town is left. The ruined church, that used to be a considerable distance inland, stands now on a beetling cliff, which is rapidly disappearing before the continued action of the waves. If I were asked to name the sleepiest and quietest place I have ever seen, it would be Dunwich. Sandwich, on the Kentish coast, where grass grows in the market-place, and dogs lie sleeping in the sun in the middle of the road, is liveliness itself compared with Dunwich. Occasionally one or two of the children and I would go and take tea with the Edwards'. Their house was only four miles distant from Southwold, and was thought by many to afford a pleasant walk over that space of shingle in the hot sun. Keene and a very old friend of his, H. Harral, the wood-engraver, were staying with the Edwards'. Keene

passed his time in sketching and practising the
bagpipes; Harral in the cheerful occupation of
digging out human bones from the cliffs, of which,
though he never secured a perfect skeleton, he
disinterred enough to make several, if the bones
had only fitted.   As we sat talking and taking our
tea at one end of the garden, Keene would march
up and down at the other playing his pipes.
Partly from nervousness, he did not care that
his audience should be in too close proximity
to him, and varied his garden walk with a stroll
on the adjacent shingle, an arrangement which, as
none of us were bagpipe enthusiasts, was satisfactory to all parties.   I have known an instance
when the sound of the pipes has not been regarded
as an unmixed blessing even by a Scotchman,

At a dinner given by Mr. John Aird, M.P.,*
at his house in town, in honour of the Scottish
painters then in London, the Queen's piper had
been engaged " to gie a skirl on the pipes " between
the courses.   A fine fellow he looked as he marched
round the table with flying tartans.   However

---

* I am happy to say I have enjoyed the friendship of Mr. Aird
and of his charming family for some years.   He is one of the most
genial and hospitable of men, and a princely patron of art.   To his
credit, he has bought every picture he has on his own unaided judgment.   His collection includes specimens of the President, Tadema,
Orchardson, Pettie, Calderon, and many others, among which I may
be allowed to mention one of mine—"An Episcopal Visitation "—a
Bishop at the Zoo inspecting the adjutant storks.

spirit-stirring such wild music may be in its native glen, accompanied by the thundering roar of mighty torrents, in a London dining-room, however large, with the windows closed, it may not be thought soothing. At all events, Pettie, who was one of the guests, was telling a humorous story. The piper passing immediately behind us gave a fearsome blast which caused the point of the tale to be lost. By the contraction of his brow and the movement of his lips, I don't think it was a benediction that Pettie uttered.

I am not able to judge of Keene's musical powers. He was one of the band of singers at Arthur Lewis's, when he lived in Jermyn Street, and afterwards at Kensington, when they were called " The Moray Minstrels." There was a vibration and tremulous quality in his voice when singing some of his favourite old songs, " The Three Ravens" or " Phillida flouts me," that I always found touching and tender. He sang as it were with tears in his voice.

Among many acts of kindness shown to me by Keene was his recommendation of me to the editor of the *Spectator*, Mr. Meredith Townsend, to whom he was related. I was installed as art critic on that journal, which post I occupied for several months, writing under the signature of " Dry Point." This made a very welcome addition to my

income, and I did my work as honestly and con-
scientiously as I was able, but never felt quite
happy in it.   I did not enjoy discussing the works
of my brethren, and would rather have written on
other subjects than art.   So it came to pass that,
as financial prospects became brighter, I resigned
my connection with the *Spectator* about the end
of 1862, having been on the staff for barely two
years.

Next door to White Cottage, Hammersmith,
where Keene lived with his mother, brother, and
two sisters, was a large old-fashioned and picturesque
garden which Keene showed me, the neighbour
who owned it being on very good terms with all
the family.   I was then wanting a background for
a picture called "The Jester's Text," and this
garden seemed to offer many useful bits and to
deserve a careful study.   Permission to work here
was readily granted, and I went each fine day to
make my study, lunching with Mrs. Keene and
her daughters.   Of this background study I afterwards made a picture of "Cowper at Olney," the
poet meditating in his garden and accompanied
by his three hares.   I was going to my work one
morning by a Hammersmith omnibus, and paid
my fare with a shilling.   The conductor gave me
a sixpence in change, worn and smooth as a piece
of glass.   I objected to take it, and asked for

another, saying, "Why, there's no image on this."
"No image on it, ain't there?" says he, giving
me another, and jumping on his monkey-board—
"You're a bloomin' image, you are! Drive on,
Bill!" I told this little episode to Keene. He
laughed, but did not see his way to make a *Punch*
drawing of it.

Charles Keene had some odd little habits.
When dining at the Arts Club or at any public
resort, he objected to conversation, and took no
part in it; but would prop his newspaper or book
against the water-bottle and read as he ate. He
never considered his breakfast complete without a
fruit tart—apple for choice. At the Arts he would
have his cup of after-dinner coffee placed on the
hob till it was nearly boiling, when he sipped it
with gusto as he smoked his seventeenth-century
"pipe of dottles," or, failing dottles, tobacco of prodigious strength. Of other beverages, tea, water, or
beer, he would never pour out any greater quantity than he could drink at one time. He had
peculiarities in his dress. I never saw him in a
great-coat, however cold the weather; he would
often wear a Scotch cap; he was generally clad
in a "suit of dittos," and nearly always carried
a small wallet slung over his shoulders, whether
walking in London streets or going to visit at a
country-house. In this wallet he managed, in some

mysterious manner, to pack such luggage as he considered necessary for a stay with his friends.

From the beginning of 1889 until the end came, Keene suffered acutely from dyspepsia and rheumatism. The deft supple hand gradually lost its power ; his form, always spare, wasted slowly away, and he became little better than a living skeleton. He would sometimes allude jocosely to his shrunken limbs. He no longer found relief or comfort in smoking ; tobacco, which he so much loved in health, was now an object of loathing, almost of horror. It was very painful to see him in these days lying on the sofa in his den, a litter of books, papers, prints, and drawings. Yet he was always cheerful, and bore his sufferings with fortitude and courage. But I have not the heart to dwell on the details of my friend's long and wearisome illness. The story is told faithfully and at length in Mr. G. Somes Layard's interesting " Life and Letters."

On a dull January morning in 1891 there was a crowd of mourners at Hammersmith Cemetery, comprising relatives and troops of friends, conspicuous among whom was the staff of *Punch*. We came away talking sadly of the loss of a friend so loyal and true, of such manly frankness and sweet simplicity of character, of the artist unequalled in his special line. The great humourist's work, scarcely acknowledged by the critics, and looked on with indifference by the public of this country, was hailed with enthusiasm abroad. It is not an exaggeration to say that Keene's reputation is European. His fame may be said to have increased since his death, and his name can never be forgotten.

CHAPTER VIII

PUNCH: ITS ART AND ARTISTS

IT has been my good fortune to have friendly relations with most of the *Punch* artists. Leech I knew, met him at Arthur Lewis's and other houses, but was never so intimate with him as with Keene or Sir John Tenniel. Of these, the leading *Punch* artists of the early sixties, the last-named of the triumvirate only remains with us. His friendship I have enjoyed for many years, and hope to enjoy that privilege for many more. My friendship for them may have influenced in some degree the estimate of their work in the critical sketch which follows, though I am unconscious that it has. With few reservations, the opinions of more than thirty years ago have been confirmed by maturer judgment, and ratified by subsequent writers. In some respects, I should rank the humour of Keene, for instance, as of higher and racier quality now, but his faculties had not then developed to their fullest extent or greatest strength.

Mr. Du Maurier was then little more than a beginner in *Punch's* pages; the vigorous work of Mr. Linley Sambourne was quite unknown, and it was at a yet later period that the facile pencil of Mr. Harry Furniss gave a novel and original treatment to political caricature. And now to the article.

"It is not my purpose to discuss the merits or record the past history of caricature in this country, but simply to offer a few remarks on that form of it which finds expression in the pages of *Punch.* In looking over the earlier volumes, now republishing, one is struck by the difference existing between the cuts in them and those which find favour now. The pages then were covered with armies of little black figures, looking as if they had been cut out of court-plaister and stuck on the white paper. One looks in vain for those subjects of contemporary domestic life (technically called 'socials,' I believe) which now form the most characteristic feature of a number of *Punch*; and though the fun of the earlier drawings is up to the present standard, in point of artistic excellence they are very far short of it. Many artists have been 'on *Punch*,' some for a few weeks, some for a few years, while others

have contented themselves with a single appearance; but we find Mr. Leech's hand busy from the
first, and he is the only one that has followed the
interests of the periodical from its commence-
ment. Kenny Meadows, Hine, Alfred Crowquill,
M'Connell, and others, have 'fretted their hour'
on the *Punch* stage. Mr. Richard Doyle's connection with it lasted for some years, and his retire-
ment is to be regretted, not only because with his
departure the element of the grotesque, in which
he so particularly excelled, vanished too, but also
because, with but few exceptions, he has since done
nothing worthy of his powers. Among these exceptions, the admirable 'Adventures of Brown, Jones,
and Robinson' must, of course, be placed; but
not the illustrations to the 'Newcomes,' nor the
'Bird's-eye Views of Society' in the *Cornhill
Magazine*. I think most people would have preferred Mr. Thackeray to illustrate his own story;
and, though the 'Bird's-eye Views' enjoy the luxury
of tinted paper, and the delicate engraving of
Dalziel Brothers, they will not in their laboured
humour compare for one moment with the fresh-
ness and droll fun of their more soberly arrayed
progenitors, 'The Manners and Customs of the
English in 1849.' But though Mr. Doyle has
quitted *Punch*, his design for the wrapper is still
continued; and every week the 'dicky bird' sur-

mounting the R D appears in company with Punch, grinning as he puts his finger to his nose, the melancholy Toby squatting on his many-volumed pedestal, and the bacchanalian procession, in which the little faun drags along by a string the mask of Brougham, a parody of an incident (not a complimentary one, by the way, to his Lordship) in Titian's great picture of 'Bacchus and Ariadne' in our National Gallery.

"The present staff of *Punch* artists consists of Messrs. Leech, Tenniel, and Charles Keene. The name of Mr. Howard must also be placed on the list. His drawings of animals, birds, and insects are, I am told, popular with the public; they may be known by the peculiarity of their style and the signature of a trident. Besides these gentlemen, there are occasional contributors, Mr. Julian Portch, Mr. G. Du Maurier, &c., &c. Foremost among all stands Mr. Leech. Connected as he has been with *Punch* from the first, he has been in a great degree instrumental in attaining and maintaining the position which it now enjoys. The heaviest blow that could fall on *Punch* would be the loss of Mr. Leech. His drawings are now the first things one looks for in opening a number. In saying this, I hope I am not wounding the feelings of any of the *Punch* writers; but it must be confessed that the letterpress has not kept

pace with the woodcuts. The comparison of the
present articles with those of the days of the
'Snob Papers' and the 'Caudle Lectures' is not
in favour of the former. For twenty years has
Mr. Leech been throwing off his brilliant and truth-
ful sketches. In them we can trace the reflex of
his mind and the gradual ripening of his humour.
He is always hearty, playful, and genial, occasionally solemn and severe, but never ill-natured,
morbid, or misanthropical. He enjoys the world
and the good it contains, and goes through life
pleasantly laughing: he has his stern moments
now and then, and fights resolutely against cant,
hypocrisy, arrogance, and vanity. Like all true
humorists, he has the pathetic faculty, and though
in the pages of a comic paper there is seldom
opportunity for its display, it peeps out now and
then with genuine effect. Mr. Leech delights in
the 'swells,' respects the poor man, but hates the
snob. He does not see much to admire or to
interest him in people whose incomes are under
£300 a year, nor can he conceive moral worth
independent of a correct aspiration of the letter *h.*
His respect for the professors of the Church, Law,
and Physic is limited, and he seems to think with
Mr. Carlyle, that when in the neighbourhood of a
bishop the safest course is to keep on the *other*
side of the hedge. The Dissenters fare no better,

and he has more than once reproduced that
Chadband and Stiggins type of character.   All
healthy manly English sports meet with ready
sympathy from Mr. Leech.   He prefers the life
of physical enjoyment to that of intellectual exertion.   The savants and blue-stockings find little
favour at his hands; the scientific man bores him;
he likes far better to be salmon-fishing with Mr.
Briggs, riding across country with Tom Noddy
and the Brookside harriers, or wading through
the turnip-fields with Tomkins after partridges 'on
the 1st.'   And what shall we say to Mr. Leech's
ladies?   As girls, they are charmingly pretty creatures, full-blown buxom beauties; but how is it,
Mr. Leech, that these very interesting young
people grow up into such repulsively ugly middle-
aged women?   Why do you so seldom represent a
lady who has attained a 'certain age' as an object
on which the eye can rest with complacency?
The elderly married lady becomes coarse-featured
and unwieldy, and the mature spinster, especially
if she have a turn for vegetarianism or marine
zoology, presents an unpleasantly angular surface,
flat feet, and rigid, meagre ankles.   But if Mr.
Leech is rather hard on middle-aged womanhood,
he has a most kindly appreciation of childhood.
How well he enters into the little aspirations and
jealousies of children, their whims, their assump-

tions of importance, their hastily struck-up friendships, and their naïve queries with which they so
frequently puzzle their elders.   He laughs gently,
too, at the boy's affectation of manly airs; his
youths have an engaging air of frank, honest good-
nature.

"The political caricatures of Mr. Leech are smart
and telling, and have that look of having been
rapidly hit off on the spur of the moment which
all work of this class should possess.   I can fancy
Lord Palmerston often chuckling over his own
portrait in *Punch*, though sometimes the joke is
too pungent to allow an 'honourable member'
with a limited sense of humour to see the joke.
Thus, Mr. Roebuck, the other day at Sheffield, was
very contemptuous about 'that thing in *Punch*,' a
drawing of Mr. Tenniel's, in which the Emperor
of Austria is running away with 'Tear'em.'   The
point evidently went home.   It is gratifying to find
that the legislative wisdom of the country does not
consider it beneath its dignity to see *Punch* for
itself, and does not find it necessary to undergo
that mysterious process suggested in the formula,
'my attention has been called,' &c., a formula
with which it appears incumbent on nine persons
out of ten who write to the *Times* to commence
their letters.   It would be tedious and needless
to enumerate Mr. Leech's most striking political

caricatures. They sound coldly in description, while much of their interest belongs necessarily to the hour of their birth. One of his most serious and impressive drawings, 'General Février turned Traitor,' the last moments of the Emperor Nicholas, with Death, in the costume of a Russian general, lifting the curtain of the dying man's bed, elicited high commendation from Mr. Ruskin.

"As regards artistic execution, everything must be said in praise of Mr. Leech. Given a certain and limited number of touches, I know of no man who can produce with them such happy results. He does not profess to be academic or elaborate, but he invariably puts the right line in the right place. He never follows out the intricacies of a fold of drapery with the definite certainty of Mr. Tenniel, or gives himself difficult problems of foreshortening or unusual attitudes, of which Mr. Keene is fond, but, as far as he professes to go, he is thoroughly right. His feeling for character and the salient points of expression is very strong, and it is very uncommon to find a caricaturist with such a perception of beauty as Mr. Leech possesses. The great George Cruikshank, with all his genius, powerful and varied as it is, has never drawn a pretty female face. Individuality is another of Mr. Leech's good qualities. We have met all his people at one time or another: his country farmers

and town swells, worldly mammas and gorgeous
footmen, his knowing horse-dealers and peculating
lodging-house keepers, his dandified hairdressers
and linen-drapers, his stout-built, red-faced old boatmen and chaffing cabmen, and those eternal plagues,
the London street-boys, are all good and true in
character.   In his wildest fun nature is never lost
sight of.   Equally happy in expression, Mr. Leech
shows us the complacent smirk of Paterfamilias as
he stands in the balcony of his seaside lodgings,
surrounded by his wife and daughters, or aghast
with horror as he breaks his first egg at breakfast
and finds himself pursued by the organ-grinders, or
smiling joyously as he bears up against the breeze,
which threatens to blow him and his daughters off
the jetty—the set grin of the French garçon—the
sad face of the man who, the morning after a white-
bait dinner at Greenwich, is asked by the page
'what fish he would like to-day?'—the terror of
the old gentleman, elaborately dressed for a dinner
party, on finding the imprint of the young street
acrobat's dirty feet on his spotless waistcoat—the
gluttonous enjoyment of the greedy boy who has
retired to a 'desolate shade' with a dozen pottles
of strawberries—the joy of the country children,
who have just discovered that by peering under
the canvas of a travelling circus they can see the
'oofs of the 'orses' for nothing—and hundreds of

others, which it would be vain to attempt parti-
cularising.   The effects of sea-sickness on the
human countenance have been well remembered
and portrayed by Mr. Leech.   A newly married
couple start for the Continent, *viâ* Boulogne,
to spend the honeymoon ; their faces are pallid,
and the eyes of Edwin have a fixed and stony
stare, admirably rendered by mere dots.   His only
chance is perfect tranquillity, but his Angelina
requests him to fetch up more shawls from the
cabin.   It is putting the love of Edwin to a severe
test.

"Mr. Leech's taste and feeling in landscape deserve special mention.   The backgrounds to his
hunting and fishing subjects reveal a watchful and
keen appreciation of nature, and, like his figures,
they have no more touches than are absolutely
necessary to secure the desired effect.   In High-
land glens and Irish lakes, in river scenes with the
swans and water-lilies, and the dense masses of
foliage under which the cows seek shelter from the
rays of the scorching sun, or the broad expanse
of meadow lands, he is equally at ease.   Hill and
dale, moor and upland, are all faithfully drawn
by his facile hand.   As a specimen of reckless
pencilling over which the hand apparently (but
not really) has had no control, but which bears
considerable resemblance to the object imitated, I

should cite Mr. Leech's drawing of a turnip-field
in the 'Almanack' for 1860.

"The works of Mr. Leech are a household word.
Combining good art with good jokes, they appeal
to all tastes and delight every class. Future anti-
quarians will revere Mr. Leech's memory for the
light he has thrown on our manners and customs.
The present generation owes him a heavy debt
in consideration of the many hearty laughs he has
afforded it. Mr. Leech should be a happy man.
He commands a large audience, and with all he
is deservedly a favourite. On my table, as I write,
are some volumes of woodcuts by Gavarni and
others of French life and character. They over-
flow with artistic cleverness and skill, but what a
moral, or rather immoral, atmosphere surrounds
them! They are devoted to the glorification of
the 'lorette,' and aim at showing the ridiculous
absurdity of regarding the marriage vow as sacred
or binding. I am glad to think that the pictures
of life and character on this side the Channel are
in purer and healthier taste, and that we can place
the works of Mr. Leech in the hands of boy or
girl without fear of causing a blush on their cheeks.
From him they will learn to admire only what is
good, upright, and manly, and to eschew all that
is vicious, mean, and heartless.

"Mr. John Tenniel, the second on our list of

Punch draughtsmen, devoted himself in his earlier days to 'high art.' His cartoons at the exhibitions in Westminster Hall will be remembered by many, and his fresco of 'St. Cecilia' may be seen any day in the New Houses of Parliament. Possessed of a very retentive memory of the form and mechanism of the human figure and the movements of animals, and having acquired the power of precise and accurate draughtsmanship at an early age, the ambition of shining as an historical painter appears suddenly to have deserted him, and in the year 1850 he joined the *Punch* staff. In looking over the volumes which contain Mr. Tenniel's work, one is struck by the peculiarity that, of all the *Punch* artists, he is the only one that has remained, as it were, stationary. His drawing is as clean and definite in his earlier illustrations as in those of to-day. With the exception that his hand has gained somewhat in freedom, there is no evidence of his having altered or modified his style in any way. The faces of Mr. Tenniel's figures (excepting always those of his political personages) have a sameness and want of individuality about them that seem to imply that he trusts rather to his extraordinary memory than to hints taken direct from nature. In the illustrations to Æsop's Fables (published in 1848), the earliest of Mr. Tenniel's wood drawings, I believe, many of the figures bear a strong family resemblance to those in *Punch*, and the present type of some of his faces may be discovered even in his Westminster cartoons. Nature, in its broad, simple sense, has received only partial study from Mr. Tenniel. The stage, the drawing academy, and the costume-book, have always intervened between him and the outer world. His sympathies are less with the present than the past. Modern dress is awkward and uncouth, and our lives deficient in romantic and picturesque incident, according to Mr. Tenniel's way of thinking. No wonder, therefore, that he seldom aims at a 'social,' or that in modern subjects he is least successful. In every species of costume he is a great and reliable authority; he portrays Greek, Assyrian, Egyptian, and North American Indian with equal fidelity. With fourteenth-century hood and liripipe, Elizabethan doublet and hose, the wig and jack-boots of Queen Anne's time, and all the manifold changes that dress has undergone in this country from the earliest to the latest times, he is perfectly acquainted. And who has drawn armour so well as Mr. Tenniel? Not a joint or rivet escapes his watchful eye. He loves to accompany the steel-clad knight when 'pricking o'er the plain,' encountering the scaly dragon, rescuing beauty in distress, or challenging all comers to a trial of skill. He revives the sports

of hunting and hawking, tilting at the ring or
quintain, and the joust and tournament, where
the 'queen of beauty and love' sits smiling amid
the clash of arms and the fanfare of trumpets,
ready to reward the victor with a laurel wreath.
In a quainter vein he shows the knight ascending
the tower of his 'ladye love' by a ladder of ropes,
while a hand holding an enormous pair of shears
issues from an arrow-slit, severs the rope, and cuts
off all chance of retreat; or when, attacking a
Moorish castle, the Moor pushes the scaling-ladder
from the wall, and the knight, to save himself from
falling, catches hold of the pagan's beard, leaving
one in doubt whether one or both will kiss their
mother earth.   One of the drollest of Mr. Tenniel's
mediæval subjects is that in which two Norman
soldiers are seen wrestling together.   Fragments of
swords, maces, and battle-axes strew the ground;
so having exhausted their stock of weapons, nothing
is left for the knights but to take each other by the
throat and struggle grimly for the fall.   Droll, too,
is the courier who blows a French horn with such
violence that the blast takes him off his feet and
sends his hat flying.   The theatrical supernumerary
—the stage ruffian who 'delights in crime,' and
whose costume consists chiefly of a broad-brimmed
hat, boots, and a buckle—and actors generally, are
great favourites of Mr. Tenniel's.   At one period

he was perpetually drawing Mr. Charles Kean, and wickedly giving undue prominence to that gentleman's nose. Mr. Tenniel must be as deeply acquainted with the equestrian play of *Mazeppa* as any of the hoarse-voiced actors who perform in that somewhat depressing drama, and no one can have a more lively appreciation of the 'points' of a Roman-nosed piebald circus-horse. His clowns, pantaloons, sprites, and acrobats are capital. Many are the clown's tricks that he has recorded in his initial letters: Clown ramming the dummy policeman in a mortar, while Pantaloon stands ready with a red-hot poker to set fire to the charge and blow the unfortunate 'Peeler' to atoms; Clown walking daintily with a hen-coop for a crinoline, to the discomfiture of the feathered brood; or carefully painting large black diagrams on the newly-washed shirts hung up to dry; and numberless others. There is humour in the notion of the cabman driven to insanity by the reduction of cab fares to the uniform rate of sixpence a mile. He has harnessed a chair, and hails imaginary passengers. He wears straws in his hair, and the walls of his cell are covered with the objectionable 'sixes,' one of which hangs in a gallows. Equally good is the howling puppy whose body is encased in a large pie labelled 'Mutton, 2d.'

"Mr. Tenniel's classic and academic feeling is

well exemplified in a series of caricatures of Flaxman's outlines which illustrate a parody on the
'Ancient Mariner,' and the 'Epsom Marbles,' a
sort of travestie of those which bear the name
of Elgin.   Punch rides gallantly along, surrounded
by his staff, literary and artistic; acrobats, gipsies,
donkey-carts, and four-in-hands follow, and the procession is closed by jockeys mounted on horses
of the Phidian rather than the racer type.   In the
title-page to vol. xxiv. (1853), Punch is throned
as Jupiter, surrounded by the lesser gods.   He
grasps pen and pencil as his thunderbolts.   His
eagle (Louis Napoleon) sits at his right.   Sir
James Graham is Neptune, and Colonel Sibthorp
Mars.   The Earl of Derby turns his back, dressed
as an acrobat; in the pose of the Farnese Hercules
he reposes on his *club* labelled 'Carlton.'   Disraeli
appears as Mercury, the speech of Thiers in his
pocket, and Britannia, with helmet-shaped bonnet,
large umbrella, and owl, is disguised as Minerva.
In his 'Dream in the British Museum,' where
the stuffed giraffe and hippopotamus jostle with
the skeleton of the mammoth and the pashts
and scarabæi of the Egyptian sculptors, or in a
'Reverie in the Crystal Palace,' where the gigantic
figures from the tomb of Abou Simbel keep watch
over the sphinxes and the Assyrian winged bull,
Mr. Tenniel gives ample proof of his powers of

fancy and imagination. Nor must his admirable
drawings of animals be overlooked. I have alluded
above to the circus-horses, but the British lion is
under great obligations to Mr. Tenniel for the
skill with which that gentleman has drawn his
portrait on numerous occasions. 'Keep Watch!'
—a double-page engraving, in which the lion of
England, having conquered the tiger of India, reposes on the body of his foe, and, looking up into
the sky, watches the contest between the eagles
of France and Austria—was not only good in political significancy, but is a grand and powerful rendering of brute form.

"But I must bid adieu to Mr. Tenniel, and only
staying to assure him that I hope the day is far
distant when we shall cease to see his quaint and
neatly-drawn figures in the pages of *Punch*, pass
on to review the drawings of Mr. Keene.

"Mr. Charles Keene has not been connected with
Punch for more than seven or eight years, but in
that time he has made visible progress. Many of
his earlier drawings are black and heavy through
over-elaboration; those of to-day, while equally
careful, are brilliant, free, and life-like. The two
chief characteristics of his style are individuality
and conscientiousness. His heads all look like
portraits, the minutest details of character are
never omitted, and every part of his drawing has

nature for its basis. Mr. Keene delights in setting himself tasks of artistic difficulty requiring much time and patience in their accomplishment. Whatever he does, he determines shall be done thoroughly. Thus, to take a common instance, in drawing a cab or cart wheel (a foreshortened one pleases him best), Mr. Keene will take care that it shall be as exactly like a wheel as he can make it, that it shall be so true in its formation that no coachmaker shall be able to find fault with it. It may not be a matter of vital importance, perhaps, to draw wheels in this careful manner in an ordinary woodcut, and Mr. Leech, whose wheels are not even round, shows that they may be drawn with the greatest recklessness. But the pleasure is the same in amount, though of a different kind, that an artist feels in looking at Mr. Leech's dashing resemblance to a wheel and Mr. Keene's actual portraiture of one. This example of the wheel may appear trivial to some readers, but is not really so. In the first place, a wheel is by no means an easy object to draw truly, and then if we find an artist so faithful in his inanimate objects, we may generally rely upon his truthfulness in higher things, such as the features and expression of men and women. Accordingly, when Mr. Keene introduces us to Buffles of the Blankshire Volunteers, he gives not only the proper number of buttons to his coat, and a faithful delineation of all his equipments, but stamps the character of the face and figure of Buffles with such force that the truth of the portrait is at once recognisable. Mr. Keene's love of outdoor nature is as strongly pronounced as Mr. Leech's. His landscape backgrounds are charmingly real. He has not that extensive knowledge of the world that Mr. Leech possesses, nor is his range of character so varied. He chiefly reproduces the dining-room waiter, the cab or omnibus driver, and the rifle volunteer. Sometimes he portrays the 'swell,' but his chief pet is the artist. Mr. Keene has depicted him under a variety of circumstances, taking in milk for his tea, writhing under the remarks of lay critics, talking 'shop' in a railway carriage, and shocking old ladies by the indifference with which he speaks of 'knocking off little girl's heads,' or moving his 'properties' and having a dispute with cabby about the lay-figure, which he wants to charge for as 'a hextra person, cos I see she was a hinvalid.' I hear of much complaint against Mr. Keene amongst the more 'select' artists for what they consider such libels on the profession! With such very thin-skinned gentlemen it would be idle to remonstrate, but a more tangible objection to Mr. Keene's artist drawings is that he only presents us with one type of the class, a being who can afford to be well, though sometimes eccentrically clad, but who prefers to paint seated on a penitential trestle in a studio, picturesque perhaps, but scarcely comfortable—a sort of carpenter's shed, which admits the wind through many a chink, and the temperature of which is scarcely rendered endurable by a stove with a perpetually smoking chimney. Mr. Keene might now and then favour us with the 'lavender kid artist' whose clothes make so capital an advertisement for his tailor, and who has a painting room in the neighbourhood of Piccadilly—the man of the day, whose talk is of dukes and countesses ; or the drawling Pre-Raphaelite, who finds every work painted by his clique 'awfully jolly,' and everything else 'awful rot ;' or the painter who attributes his want of success to his ill-luck instead of to his bad work, and considers that the Royal Academicians, unanimous for once in their lives, have leagued themselves into a conspiracy to crush him.

"Political caricature is never attempted by Mr. Keene. He confines himself to conversational subjects, initial letters, and headings to the prefaces and indexes. His jokes are sometimes laboured, and not always obvious. Judging from other illustrations by Mr. Keene, such as the admirable series to the 'Good Fight'* in *Once a Week*, I

* Since republished as "The Cloister and the Hearth," by Charles Reade.

should say his genius is grave rather than gay. But he can be humorous when he likes.   There is grotesque drollery in the group of gorillas which heads the preface to the last volume, and many others might be mentioned did space permit.   Mr. Keene's present style is large, broad, and energetic. He draws with firmness and power, improving gradually but surely, though sometimes his progress is marked by leaps.   One of these leaps took place two weeks ago, in a drawing of two artists on stilts, which, regarded from an artistic point of view, is perhaps the best Mr. Keene has achieved. Sea, beach, boats, and figures are drawn with a light but certain hand, while the brilliant sunny effect deserves the highest praise.   I have never seen a picture bearing Mr. Keene's name, and am told he does not paint.   It is a pity, for he is evidently the owner of great pictorial power.   The demands on his time are doubtless great, but he surely does not lack the inclination to paint, and if he has the inclination, can he not contrive to shape the opportunity?   It is out of no disrespect to Mr. Keene's *Punch* drawings, but because I think so highly of them, that I believe him capable of finer art, and, in common with many others, should be glad to find the name of Charles Keene in the Royal Academy catalogue for 1862.

" Respecting Mr. Howard's ornithological and

animal drawings, I have but little to say in praise.
They are small and hesitating in execution, but
give the idea of a man who is perfectly satisfied
with his own performances. Mr. Julian Portch
draws with a pretty touch and dainty pencil. Mr.
G. du Maurier has not been sufficiently long before
the public to estimate him truly, yet his drawings
have a pleasant silvery look, and exhibit refinement
and gentlemanly feeling. If he continues to improve as he has lately, *Punch* will have found in
Mr. du Maurier a great acquisition."

CHAPTER IX

THE ST. JOHN'S WOOD CLIQUE

SKETCH OF ME BY HERKOMER.

A PICTURE called "The Jester's Text" was the last I painted in the little house in Camden Town, and not long after it was hung on the walls of the Royal Academy we left that neighbourhod for the more congenial regions of St. John's Wood, where Calderon, Leslie, Hodgson, and Storey already resided.

D. W. Wynfield lived with his mother and sisters on the Paddington side of Edgware Road, and W. F. Yeames, on his return from the Continent, where in Russia and Italy his early life had been passed, took a studio in the same thoroughfare. These seven were the original members of the St. John's

146

Wood Clique—Calderon, Leslie, Hodgson, Yeames, Wynfield, Storey, and myself. Clique was an ill-chosen name, perhaps, but it was adopted thoughtlessly. Others talked of us as the St. John's Wood School. This was not a correct definition, either, of what was really a bond of brotherhood. "The Gridirons" was another name we gave ourselves, and this was the best, and most descriptive of our object in forming this band, which was, while continuing to be the best of friends, to criticise each other's works in the frankest and most unsparing manner. This is what he whom I must always consider the head of the Clique (Calderon) said at the time of our formation : "We have all of us now to work together, and do our very best, not caring who is first or last, but helping each other, so that all may come out strong. The better each man's picture, the better for all." In a short time the Clique became an established fact, and was recognised as such by the public press—though not always with enthusiasm.

A writer in *Fraser's Magazine* for July 1864, in an article reviewing the Academy for that year, wrote at some length on the St. John's Wood Clique, and used these words : "In speaking of this group of artists as the 'coming men,' we have intended to indicate a fact, not to express an adhesion on our part." But it is not my intention to discuss the artistic merits of the Clique. It is rather late in the day to do that : I prefer to be the chronicler of their social acts. The relation of these will, I trust, afford more amusement to my readers than any dissertation on their art which I could offer them.

In course of time a few honorary members were added to the number of the Clique. These were F. Walker, G. du Maurier, Val Prinsep, and Eyre Crowe. We designed and had engraved a gridiron, with the motto "Ever on thee," for our notepaper, &c., of which this woodcut is an enlarged version. The badge or order was a miniature brass gridiron, worn in the button-hole on all ceremonial or mock ceremonial occasions, as the installation of an associate or honorary member.

In the earlier years of the Clique, we would meet in the morning, after sending in our work to the Academy, and take a good country walk. We bought provisions on the road, leaving them at some roadside inn to be cooked by our return.

The old " Spotted Dog " at Neasden was a favourite resort. Returning at an appointed hour, we discussed our chops and sausages, and, if the weather was fine, would aid digestion afterwards by a gentle innocuous game of bowls on the tavern green, returning to St. John's Wood by dusk. As our circumstances improved, we went farther afield ; a little trip by rail would be indulged in, and more elaborate though still humble meals at the principal inn of the town we visited. On these days out, one of the members of the Clique stood treat, paying all expenses except that of the railway journey. The idea of these days originated with Leslie, who led off in July 1862 with a trip to St. Albans, and its fine old Abbey, of which the restorations had not then commenced. Nothing calling for special remark occurred that day. We dined at the " Peahen," then, and possibly now, kept by people of the same name as myself, but not related, so far as I know, to the writer. Not that I would vouch for the fact ; for the Marks's have increased and multiplied in a marvellous manner. I have more cousins than I know of, or care to count : many I have never seen, nor am I ever likely to see them.

The second day was given by Calderon. Walker was by this time an honorary member of the Gridirons, for he was one of the party. We spent the earlier part of the day in Cassiobury Park,

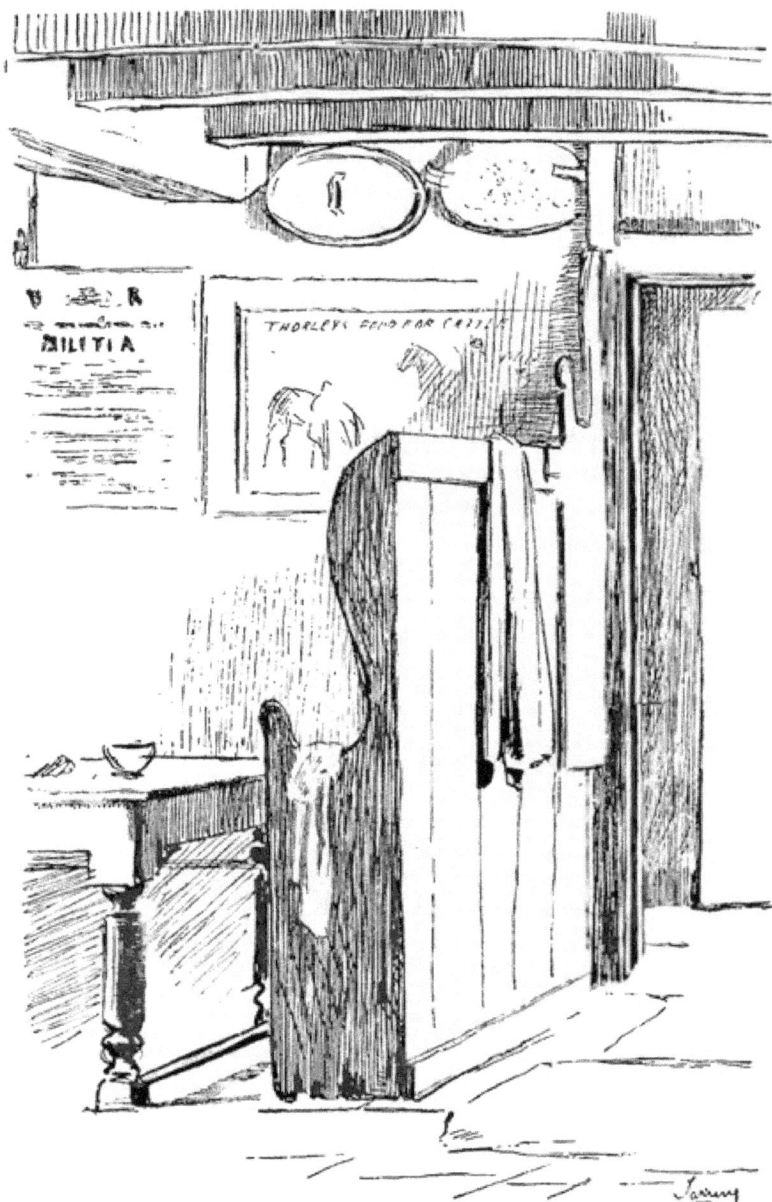

THE "TAP" OF A COUNTRY "PUB."

and, among other amusements, got up a swimming-match between Yeames and Walker. Both performed in the most Beckwith-like manner, and the race was a dead-heat. We dined at the Lord Essex Arms, Watford. When the cloth was cleared, Calderon's health was proposed and drank in what beverage history telleth not, but it certainly was not champagne. I then sang some verses in honour of our host, written for the occasion, but kept dark till the proper moment, to ensure their effect. They are somewhat personal, but my friend is good-natured enough to allow me to print an extract. The air, an old English one, will be found in "Chappell's Ballads," and was selected as being doleful and appropriate to the general sentiment.

CALDERON'S HEALTH.

Air.—" *The moon shall be in darkness.*"

I.

Of all the lucky fellows
Who bask in fortune's sunshine,
None compare with Philip Calderon,
An old friend of mine ;
And though in the country
He's brought us out to tea,
Don't let us cease to growl at
His pop-u-lar-i-tee !

2.

For twelve long years I've known him,
Ere his beard was yet well grown,
When he was thinner than a lath,
And came out strong in bone;
Then we studied art together
Under dear old Mr. Leigh,
And picked up a few wrinkles
Chez Picot à Paree!

3.

For ev'ry study that he made,
I finished at least four,
And while he loafed so merrily,
I always laboured sore;
What "cost me a groaning,"
He did quite easily,
And in language strong I oft described
His great fa-cil-i-tee!

4.

But I don't his course by tracing
Your anger wish to rouse,
You all know what rot he painted,
And its climax—"Broken Vows."
Yet since that time he's gone on
Improving rapid-lee,
And is hailed the next Associate
Of the Royal A-cad-e-mee!

ELECTION OF A.R.A.'S, 1864.

5.

I end my song by wishing him
Wealth, titles, honours, fame,
And may he prosper long and well
In life's arduous up-hill game ;
And may he ne'er forget the friends
Who don't get on like he,
But give them all a treat sometimes,
And take them out to tea !

The metre is here and there elastic, but all came right in the singing. Verse four was prophetic. Calderon was not the next Associate actually, but in 1864—a year after the date of this day—achieved that honour in company with F. Leighton, now president, and E. B. Stephens, the late sculptor.

Yeames was host on the next occasion, when we went to Walton-on-Thames and Shepperton. This, I think, was the time when, once fairly out of Waterloo Station, we proceeded to get ourselves up as if we had been severely injured in some football or cricket-match, or other athletic sport. When we alighted at Walton, one had a patch over his eye, one walked lamely with two sticks, another with one ; there were some arms in slings. I bought a quartern loaf, and Crowe a plum-cake. Leslie and Walker playing on tin whistles headed this procession of cripples, which walked, limped,

and hobbled into Shepperton. Though amused
and puzzled, the people we met or passed refrained
from chaff or jeers. One old lady, however, who
saw through our shamming, reproved us by saying, "Ye ought to be ashamed of yourselves—you
might be struck so!"

When we got to a convenient place, the whistles
ceased playing, and I addressed the natives, assuring
them that I was to be Member for the borough
at the next election, and when that happy day
arrived, the quartern loaf, such as I showed them,
would be greatly reduced in price—in fact, all but
given away. Crowe then cut up the plum-cake,
and distributed the slices among the assembled
children. We then hobbled away to a less
populous spot—"a more removed ground,"—got
rid of our complaints, and again became, in out-
ward appearance at least, something like rational
beings. We had other holidays together, but none,
so far as I remember, in which there was such exu-
berant fooling. At Farningham—one of Leslie's
days—Yeames and Storey had a foot-race in the
shallow little Darent, without shoes or stockings.
As the bottom was covered with broken bottles
and sharp stones, this rash proceeding might have
been attended with dangerous consequences; but
fortunately no feet were cut nor tendons divided.
To be young is to be thoughtless.

On the return journey, at each station we stopped, I harangued the people, asking, among other questions, if there were "any lady or gentleman for the diving-bell." The guard came up to our carriage, and addressing me, said, "Well, sir, you are a cure!"

The last of these days was given by Walker. Always ambitious to be first in whatsoever he undertook, he allowed zeal to outrun discretion, and by the sumptuous and costly nature of his entertainment, put all previous ones into the shade, and precluded members of the Clique from giving another in future. It was a fine old-fashioned April morning that we of the gridiron met at Walker's house in St. Petersburgh Place, where a private bus and a pair of greys awaited us. We drove to and lunched at Hampton Court, and had a costly dinner at the Castle, Richmond, with champagne galore. With the best, most generous, but mistaken intention, Walker thus put the extinguisher on these pleasant days, for it was found impossible after this to return to the old simplicity.

On Sunday mornings the Clique was in the habit of assembling at Calderon's studio, and, if the weather were fine, walking to Willesden, Neasden, and sometimes to Hendon. Our most frequent route was, I think, along West End Lane, then a rural solitude, now populous and covered

with the abortions of the jerry-builder. One
winter season the Sunday mornings were devoted
to the decoration of the walls of Hodgson's painting-room, which was not a regular studio, but two
ordinary rooms knocked into one. The house,
which still exists, was then known as 5 Hill Road,
Abbey Road. The road has since been re-
numbered. The subjects painted were all Shakespearian, with one exception. The figures were a
little under life-size. The walls were covered with
paper, and coloured in distemper of a uniform
greenish-grey tint. On this ground the decorations
were painted in oil colour, in flat tones, with the
least possible amount of shadow, and a definite
outline. Leslie painted the duel scene from
Twelfth Night; Storey, Katherine and Petruchio.
A scene from the *Tempest*, and Touchstone and
Audrey fell to my share. The most elaborate
composition, Rosalind, Celia, and Orlando after
the wrestling in *As You Like It*, was by Yeames.
Calderon occupied a space over the fireplace
with portraits of Hodgson and Mrs. Hodgson in
Elizabethan costume. It is a long time since I
saw these works. Hodgson eventually built a
studio adjoining his house, and the decorated room
was devoted to domestic requirements; but when I
last saw them, some years after they had been
executed, they were in excellent condition, had

neither faded nor become lower in tone, but were as fresh and bright as they looked when first finished.

In our summer Sunday-morning rambles we often met the late Mr. Herbert, R.A., either on foot or driving a small pony phaeton, accompanied by Mrs. Herbert. As he walked or drove slowly along, he would discuss art and its professors in a half-humorous, half-oracular manner, rendered piquant by the adoption of a French accent, which was characteristic of him in later years. This and other little eccentricities had become by continual habit a second nature. In talking of some of the younger artists, he would say, "There is a great deal of meat in that young man's pie;" of another, who could not conceal his desire to get into the Academy, he remarked, "That man blows his trumpet too loud;" and described one who too palpably imitated the style of a well-known Academician as "an antelope of the desert endeavouring to walk in the footsteps of the lion. He may tread in them, but the footprints are not the same." Mourning apparel he called "the livery of death," and described a cat as "a little animal of the tiger species, that you keep in your houses." More witty was his assertion that the principal figure in Michael Angelo's "Last Judgment" "is not our Lord, but a convulsive Jupiter." He spoke of

the "Renaissance" with horror, and would counsel
the young painter to avoid studying at Rome.
"He may get honey from the flowers, but is more
likely to get poison than honey."

One afternoon, Calderon and I came upon Herbert in the shop of an artist's colourman, with
whom many of the painters dealt. He was selecting brushes—nodded recognition to us, and, having
made his choice, said to the colourman, "You
will send me these, then, to-morrow morning; do
not forget." Pausing for a moment, he continued,
"I had a cab somewhere," looked round the shop,
even under the counter; but not finding it, a
sudden thought struck him. "Ah! it is outside.
Good-bye!" and pressing our hands to his heart,
as was his custom, he vanished into his four-
wheeler. Once the French accent was dropped
for a moment. Herbert was complaining of his
treatment by the Hanging Committee in some
particular year. "I sent a picture—a brown picture—and they hung it against a brown door"—
(then in pure English undefiled), "the scoundrels!"
Sir Edwin Landseer and Herbert were neighbours on opposite sides of the St. John's Wood
Road, and would play billiards together at Sir
Edwin's house. One evening whisky-punch was
produced, and a glass being handed to Herbert,
he tasted it, smacked his lips, and his thoughts

being in Paris as usual, said, "What is this? It is
good. We don't have it; but if we knew it, we
should have it." "What are you sending to the
Academy?" inquired Sir Edwin. "Oh, not much!
a little thing, about as large only as your billiard-
table." One evening he was walking home with
Landseer from the Athenæum Club. He saw a
poor woman. "Stay a bit; I want to perform a
charity. Can you lend me a sixpence?" Presently
they came across another beggar woman, when Herbert exclaimed, " I must perform another charity!
Have you another sixpence? But no; you shall do
the charity this time; it will be good for your soul!"

Herbert was one of the best and most amusing
talkers I have met among members of the Academy.
When he left his house in St. John's Wood
Road, he went to live at the Chimes, Kilburn,
built for him by the younger Pugin. Pettie lived
for some years in the old house opposite to what
was once Landseer's, and since inhabited by H. W.
B. Davis, R.A. Being such close neighbours, I
saw a great deal of Pettie, and we became very
intimate. On the night of his election as full member, some twenty years ago, we left the Academy
together, when he asked me to convey the news
to his family, as he had some business to see after
on the way, which would occupy but a short time,
when he would follow me. I readily consented. On

reaching his house, I found his wife, his father, and mother quietly awaiting the news, for his election was a foregone conclusion. Mrs. Marks was also present. I suggested we might have a bit of fun in welcoming the new R.A. There was no time to be lost, for he might come in at any moment. Some laurel leaves were hastily gathered from the garden and made into a wreath. It had scarcely been completed when we heard Pettie's footsteps.

My wife struck up "See the conquering hero comes!" with a comb and curl-paper, and Pettie on entering the room was at once crowned with laurel. As soon as there was some cessation in the merriment, I made a speech, proposing the health and long life of the newest Academician, the toast being drank in Scotch whisky and water. Pettie replied with the only speech I ever heard him make. At this distance of time, I cannot pretend to give it verbatim, but remember in the course of it he used something like the following words :—"When I first came up to London, I had some vague idea of avenging Flodden, but I soon found everybody was so kind, so hearty, and so hospitable, that the idea grew fainter and fainter every day, and after awhile it disappeared, and I had no wish to avenge Flodden at all." Poor Pettie! he died at the comparatively early age of fifty-four. A kinder heart, a more generous nature, a friend more loyal and true, would be hard to find.

CHAPTER X

IT was a brilliant and splendid idea which occurred to three members of the Clique to rent a mediæval castle to live and work in. In whose brain the idea originated I am not certain, but the project was carried out by Calderon, Yeames, and Wynfield in the summer of 1866, when they took Hever Castle, Kent, for three months. Calderon, with his wife and young family ; Yeames, who had been lately married, with his wife ; and Wynfield, the bachelor of the party, with such servants as were necessary, migrated from the smoke and conventional houses of London to the pure air and romantic surroundings of a castellated mansion.

Hever is of the reign of Edward III., when domestic architecture may be said to have arisen in England, and, though comfort and elegance were sought after, security was not forgotten.

Although altered, added to, and modernised at different times, Hever retains much of its form and character as when originally built. It is distant from the Edenbridge station of the South Eastern Railway about three miles, and can be reached by a pleasant walk from the village along lanes and field-paths. It lies so low that you are scarcely aware of a castle till you are close upon it. The site may have been selected from its proximity to the River Eden, which gives facilities for surrounding the building by a moat. The appearance of the castle is striking and picturesque; quadrangular in form, it encloses a courtyard. The original drawbridge is replaced by a fixed wooden one; the moat remains. The principal front is the fortified part, consisting of a lofty gate-house flanked by two square towers. This was the only entrance to the castle, and the architect has exerted all his skill in its defence. Over the gateway are machiolations, from which missiles could be showered on the heads of assailants. The towers are pierced with loopholes, through which arrows might be discharged without much chance of similar compliments being returned. Three stout gates and portcullises are arranged one behind the other within the gateway. Above the guard-rooms in the gate-house are chambers provided with furnaces for melting lead and pitch,

with which to give a warm reception to would-be
intruders, and all other defensive appliances were
carefully provided for those who persisted in calling after being warned you were "not at home."
Hever owes its celebrity, however, less to feats of
arms and warlike recollections, than to its having
been the abode of two of the wives of that much-
married monarch, Henry VIII. It was the residence of Anne Boleyn; and after his divorce from
Anne of Cleves, he granted Hever Castle and
manor to her as long as she should remain in
England.   Of the interior little need be said; there
is the great hall, the original state-room of the
castle; the dining-hall, with long tables and benches
and huge fireplace; the "grand" staircase, leading
to the chapel and gallery or ball-room, long and
low, with walls and ceilings of panelled oak, and,
among others, a scantily furnished room, called
Anne Boleyn's bedroom, with the actual bed—so
tradition says—on which she slept, though I don't
think much faith ought to be wasted on the legend.

It was here, then, the three friends spent their
time pleasantly and profitably, painting each day,
except on the one reserved for visitors, and getting
through a considerable amount of work.   Among
other "bits," Calderon painted the courtyard,
which afterwards formed the background of his
picture "Home after Victory," and Yeames made a

"Haunted Chamber" out of Anne Boleyn's bed-room, with two ladies in modern riding-habits startled by the noise made by some rats scuttling among the yellow bed-hangings. Storey stayed there some weeks, and painted a humorous picture which he called, "After you, sir,"—two cavaliers standing before a door leading from the courtyard, each begging the other to precede him. No special work of Wynfield's occurs to me, but he painted some backgrounds and photographed others. He was a very good and painter-like photographer. His series of heads of artists, in characteristic hoods, caps, and bonnets, were quite new at that time in the art.

After they had got settled down in their new abode, the custodians of the castle invited the rest of the Clique to "spend a happy day" there. So down we went accordingly. Du Maurier and Crowe were of the party, but I'm not sure if Walker or Prinsep accompanied us. It was while making preparations for the entertainment of the guests that the dining-hall chimney caught fire, which naturally caused alarm and anxiety. What if any catastrophe should happen to so interesting a monument of bygone days? No amount of in-surance could replace so interesting a relic. And while some ran for water, and others for blankets, and some ascended to the roof to stifle the fire with

mats and other persuaders, bang! the sound of
an explosion was heard! The maids screamed and
others were startled, but the cause was soon discovered. The gardener had shot his gun up the
chimney, which probably not having been swept
for years, discharged volumes of soot on the
pavement of the hall. House-flannels and water
soon made the hearth and its surroundings pre-
sentable again, and all was once more peace and
equanimity.

The next day we took train to Edenbridge, and
walked from the station. Our arrival was not proclaimed by the blare of trumpets, nor was any
guard of buff-coated retainers assembled on the
drawbridge in our honour; no standard floated idly
in the noon-tide breeze, nor were any "ordnance
shot off within." But our welcome was hearty all
the same, if of the fashion of the nineteenth century.
After looking about the grounds and a few of the
more remarkable rooms, we sat down to lunch, or
rather to the banquet, in the spacious dining-hall,
not "served up by sewers and seneschals," but by
neat-handed Phyllises, quiet arrangements in black
and white, more ornamental and more noiseless in
their movements than any bevy of blue-coated
serving-men would have been. The meal finished,
and the harmless necessary smoke enjoyed, we
went over the rest of the castle, loafed about

the grounds, while some amused themselves with croquet (lawn-tennis was then unknown). In short, it was just "go as you please."

A small punt floated in the moat, of which Storey and I took possession, having first removed shoes and stockings, for the bottom boards were wet and slippery. Storey was the puntist, and guided the craft to the different groups of men on the banks, whom I sprinkled with water from the punt's bailer. But retribution was in store, and my frolic soon cut short. An unexpected movement of the punt made me lose my balance and I toppled over and fell backwards into the moat, amid roars of laughter from the men and a little scream or two from the ladies. No part of me was visible save my feet, by which I held on, or rather by my heels, and, aided by Storey, who stretched out the saving hand as he balanced the punt, I regained an upright position, and, dripping with water, ran to the castle and put on a suit of Calderon's clothes. This was easy enough twenty-five years ago; though several inches shorter, I was not much stouter than Calderon, my fighting weight being only 10 stone 8 lbs. Except that the legs and arms of my new garments were inconveniently long, the general aspect was worthy of a tailor's dummy or the latest addition to Madame Tussaud's. The rest of the day passed without excitement, beyond the mild joys of

croquet, until the time for our return to town.   It
was deemed prudent that, as damp might still be
hanging about my own clothes, I should continue
to wear Calderon's.   This saved rheumatism, but
at the cost of paying the fare to town.   The half of
my return ticket, a dried pulp, was found next
morning in my own waistcoat pocket.

I went again for a day to Hever before the
tenancy of my friends expired, with one or two
other Gridirons, and slept the night there.   I half
hoped I might be rewarded with the sight of a
ghost of some former occupant of the building ;
but no such luck.   Perhaps the season was un-
favourable to displays of the supernatural.   Being
summer-time, there was no fire timed to burn
dimly, if I should wake at ten o'clock, nor was
there any tapestry to be put in motion by drafts
of air, or to be drawn aside by the white skinny
hand of the late lamented.   As I had extinguished
the candle on getting into bed, there was little
chance of its burning with a blue flame.   Shall I
ever see a ghost ?   Life is short, and is a running
rather than a walking shadow, when sixty years
have been past.   If any departed shade wishes to
make my acquaintance, it is time to "hurry up."

When in my twenties, I was on a walking tour
with a friend in Kent and Surrey, and one night
after I had retired to my room, I did think for a

moment I was going to be favoured with the sight of something uncanny at least. I had always been told, when in a strange place, to look under the bed before getting into it. I did so, and saw a pair of horns and hoofs. Startled for one moment, the next showed me they were too small in size for " Auld Clootie's ; " they belonged to the stuffed body of a roebuck, which had been placed and left there for some unknown reason.

The editor of *Punch* paid a visit to Hever while Calderon and Co. were there. He had telegraphed in the morning to announce his coming. On arriving at Edenbridge in the late afternoon, he ordered a carriage at the inn to take him over. They asked him, would he kindly take charge of a telegram for the castle which had arrived that morning. Mr. Burnand found it to be his own ; and on reaching that manorial pile, he with considerable difficulty managed to knock up the inmates, who, having gone to bed at an early hour, were in their first sound sleep. All this, and more, Mr. Burnand has told in his well-known witty manner in one of his " Happy Thoughts " series.

Each member of the Clique, with the exception of Storey, was a volunteer in the early sixties. I think Leslie was the first to join the movement, and was one of the Victoria Rifles. D. W. Wynfield was the next; he enlisted in the Artists' Corps,

then the 38th Middlesex; Phillips, the portrait-
painter, son of the Academician, commanding.
Wynfield was a most enthusiastic volunteer, and
devoted a great deal of time to the business of
the corps.   He induced Yeames and Hodgson to
become recruits.   Calderon and I were more shy,
and inclined at first to ridicule the whole movement, but eventually thought better of it; and one
afternoon, during the hours appointed for drill,
having let no one know of our intention, presented
ourselves at head-quarters and were duly sworn in,
to the surprise and amusement of the others.   Old
Burlington House was our head-quarters, and the
drills took place in the gardens where the Royal
Academy and the learned Societies now have their
homes.   The Artists' was a very different corps in
those days to what it has since become under the
fostering care of Sir F. Leighton, Val Prinsep, and
especially of Colonel Edis.   It is not unusual now
for musters to be over 500 men in strength.   Then
the numbers might be reckoned by fives, or even
units.   A field-day was proposed for Wimbledon,
for instance; we would parade at Burlington House,
but so ashamed used we to be of the smallness of
our numbers, that we dared not face, as a body,
the chaff of the rude street-boy or of the raucous-
voiced rough, but divided ourselves into twos and
threes, and sneaked down to Waterloo Station,

avoiding observation as much as possible by going along bye-streets. As numbers increased, we put

MARKS AS A VOLUNTEER.
Drawn by F. J. Skill.

on a bolder front, and would march along in a compact if not very numerous body, headed by

our buglers blowing lustily and long. Many
bloodless field-days did we enjoy together, and
in all weathers. Of these, the Easter reviews at
Brighton remain most in the memory. The trudging through the dusty furrows of ploughed fields,
scorched by the sun and dried by the east wind
(the wind was always in the east on these days);
the occasional halts, when the cold wind would
refrigerate your back as the hot sun would burn
your face; the file and volley firing, in which an
occasional ramrod would be shot off (no breech-
loaders then), and the delightful incomprehensibility
of the manœuvres, or as much of them as one
was able to see, are all pleasant to think of. I
remained over seventeen years in the corps, and
in most of them was efficient, doing the annual
number of drills. I never was good at shooting,
never became a marksman, which I attribute more
to nervousness than to short-sight. The moment
I pointed my rifle at the target, I began to tremble
all over, and made a very fair number of ducks-
eggs. I might have had promotion in the corps,
but my ambition did not lie that way. I tried a
corporalship for some little while, but found I was
less independent even with that humble title, and
retired into the comfortable obscurity of the ranks
as a full private.

Wynfield, on the other hand, put his whole heart

into volunteering, and got promoted gradually. He went through all the necessary duties—a month's drill with the regulars, &c.—and eventually became captain. He died, poor fellow, of consumption in May 1877, thus making the first break in the Clique brotherhood. We followed him to his last resting-place in Highgate Cemetery.

My last appearance as a volunteer was at the annual inspection of the Artists' Corps in June 1879, which took place on the parade-ground in front of the Horse Guards. My eldest son was present in the rear rank. The rain came down heavily and without intermission the whole time of the ceremony; we got drenched to the skin. The unusual—I may say unique—spectacle was presented on that day of a Royal Academician and his son as privates in the ranks of a volunteer corps. After this touch of pride which aped humility I retired. I had a very kind and genial letter from my captain, Val Prinsep, expressive of his regret that I found it necessary to take such a step.

A record of the Clique would be scarcely complete without reference to an Exhibition with which they were connected, as members of committee or exhibitors, or in both capacities. This had the awkward name of "The General Exhibition of Water Colour Drawings," and was formed by a number of artists and amateurs in 1864. They considered that no sufficient opportunities were afforded for the exhibition of drawings by artists who were not members of the " Old " Water Colour Society or of the " New " Society. It was known colloquially as " The Dudley Gallery," in consequence of the old masters belonging to Lord Ward having been exhibited there previous to the formation of " The General Exhibition." The "gallery" was dropped eventually, and it became simply "The Dudley."

The venture was a success from the first, and really did supply a long-felt want, unlike many projects and schemes which profess to do so. There were many good names on the original committee, of which I may mention those of J. B. Burgess, Frank Dillon, W. S. Coleman, H. Moore, E. J. Poynter, the two Severns (Arthur and Walter), Tom Taylor, and Frank Walton. Dr. Edward Hamilton was treasurer, and G. L. Hall, since dead, honorary secretary.

It must have been in 1866 that J. E. Hodgson, Leslie, Wynfield, Yeames, and myself joined the committee by invitation. Calderon and Storey, though not members, were constant contributors to the exhibitions. The committee, or rather the workers of that body, were energetic, and gave up a large amount of time to their duties, which included

being present on the days of sending in, relieving
each other in batches to receive the works, entering each one in a book, pasting a corresponding
number on each, selecting, and finally arranging
the whole upon the walls.   The expenses were

COMMITTEE MEETING CARD AS FINALLY DECIDED ON.

kept as low as possible ; these included the services
of a secretary, of two or three commissionaires who
acted as porters, and of the workmen who did the
actual hanging.

The selection of the works being the easiest
as well as the most amusing part of the business,

always attracted a goodly number of the committee,

GENERAL EXHIBITION OF WATER COLOUR DRAWINGS.
GENERAL MEETINGS OF THE COMMITTEE.
188
DAY, APRIL   DAY, DEC.ᴿ
6·P.M.
BY ORDER
R·F· McNAIR, SEC.

FIRST IDEA OF CARD, GIVING DATES OF COMMITTEE MEETINGS OF THE "DUDLEY."

who sat at or stood round a long trestled table.
The president of the day had the book before him

with the numbers, and marked in the columns alongside A, D, or R, according as the voting went. I
may state for the benefit of the unlearned that A
stands for accepted, D for doubtful, R for rejected.

	A.	D.	R.
J. Smith	...	...	R
R. Brown	...	...	...
T. Jones	...	D	...

As the president marked in the book D or R, so
did the committee-man on the back of the drawing,
the R in his hands becoming an X. It is only in
novels or other works of fancy that A is ever
marked on a picture. I have called the "selection" of works amusing. Though at other exhibitions at which I have assisted it has been a grave
and anxious task, it was undertaken at "The
Dudley" in the most light-hearted way. Silence
was not compulsory, and the jest or snatch of song
would be heard occasionally during the examination of the works.

Those who have never been present at a similar
ceremonial have no idea of the frightful mass of
incompetent rubbish that the hapless jurymen have
to look through. Youths of both sexes send their
earliest efforts, acting under the impression that
"anything will do for the Dudley." A rush of
bad pictures would come, which would be crossed

M

at the rate of thirty a minute. It is only the "doubtful" works that require lengthened consideration. The good are hailed with acclamation, the bad dismissed instantly with howls.

The Exhibition of 1869 was the first in which every member of the Clique was represented, Calderon sending a drawing in *guache* on canvas which attracted much attention.

As the Water Colour Exhibition only occupied the spring months of the year, it was determined to have another of cabinet works in oil in the winter. This was carried out under the management of the same committee. Both this and the Water Colour show brought many a painter to the front. The Dudley was a nursery-ground for young artists who have since blossomed into fame. Briton Rivière and Miss Thompson, now Lady Butler, were among the early contributors. Whistler exhibited at the oil show, but he had made his name some years before. Academicians and members of the two Water Colour Societies would frequent the Dudley, and take stock of the painters who were coming on. Leslie thought his election as A.R.A. was materially assisted by the exhibition of his picture "The Rose-Harvest," while my admission to the ranks of the dear "Old Water Colour Society" was entirely due to having a drawing on the walls in the spring of 1871, a portly monk complacently looking at a group of pigs in a beech forest, called "Thoughts of Christmas."

Between the closing of the Water Colour Exhibition and the opening of the one for cabinet oils there were some months available, and these were devoted, as far as I can remember, about 1874 to an exhibition of works in monochrome, or " Black and White," as it was called.   I think I am correct in stating that this was the first of the kind, held not only at the Dudley, but in the United kingdom.   It excited the greatest interest among artists by the high standard of the work, and came as a revelation to the public by its novelty and excellence.   Some of the best French artists also contributed etchings and drawings, and Whistler some of his excellent work.   I have no catalogue by me, and am unable to give the names of the principal exhibitors.   The great feature of the show was about a hundred drawings on wood blocks and on paper, lent by the proprietors of the *Illustrated London News* and the *Graphic* newspapers.   All of them of great merit, there were some that by the excellence of their technique and brilliant execution "quite took one's breath away," as was said to me by a distinguished painter, whom I had the honour of conducting round the Exhibition.   It seemed that cleverness and dexterity had here reached their extreme limits.   But this was

nearly twenty years ago. Since then the standard
of excellence has been raised steadily and continually, "for emulation hath a thousand sons,
that one by one pursue." "Process" is supplanting
wood engraving, and we have the *Daily Graphic*,
which has become one of the many wonders of
illustrated journalism for excellent work and rapid
production.

It was in the year 1882 that the old Dudley
came to an end; many members of the committee
were drafted into the Institute of Painters in Water
Colours, and swelled the ranks of what used to be
the New Water Colour Society.

Exhibitions are, however, still held at the gallery
in Piccadilly under the auspices of the "Dudley
Gallery Art Society," of which Mr. Walter Severn
is President.

Such is the history of the St. John's Wood
Clique. Six of the original members still exist,
but one only remains in the neighbourhood. The
first break in the little band was occasioned by
the death of D. W. Wynfield, on the 26th May
1887, at his house in Grove End Road. His last
picture, "Whittington's Banquet," was hung in
the Academy of that year, in gallery No. VI.
After death came removals. The first to go was
George Leslie, who migrated to Wallingford with
his wife and family, where he combines the life

of a painter with that of a country gentleman,
except that he is not what is commonly called a

Mallet on 9 1/2 o clock

Note of invitation from Hodgson
April 10 1865.—

sportsman, as he finds more pleasure in the con-
templation and studying of Nature's works than in

their destruction.   Calderon followed next.   He was
elected Keeper of the Academy, if not in 1887, at

THE ST. JOHN'S WOOD CLIQUE.   (*Photographed by Wynfield.*)

least in the following year, when his name appears
for the first time in the catalogue as " Keeper and
Trustee."   A few years later J. E. Hodgson set

up his tent near the picturesque old town of Amersham. Storey moved to Hampstead. Yeames has recently taken a house some little distance from town. The writer of these pages is therefore the only one remaining in the neighbourhood which gave birth to the Clique, and in which he trusts, under Providence, to end the remainder of his days.

The accompanying photograph, taken by D. W. Wynfield in 1864 or 1865, gives portraits of the seven members of the Clique. Commencing at the left, his hands resting on a croquet mallet, is Calderon ; then Yeames, Leslie, Marks, Hodgson, and Storey ; the seated figure to the right is Wynfield, the only member who never became A.R.A. or R.A. It is rather singular that the six others obtained academic honours exactly in the order in which they are shown in the photograph.

Hornbill.

CHAPTER XI

A MONG the many figures that are associated with my memories for many years, that of Arthur J. Lewis is one of the most prominent. No man had a wider acquaintance with artists than he. He was, and is, the companion and friend of all the painters of his time, from Millais downwards. Not a professional artist himself, he is an amateur of considerable and varied talent. He was a constant worker at the Langham Friday sketching evenings, had a picture at every Academy Exhibition for many years, and was an etcher of skill and taste. In this latter capacity he was the promoter of the Junior Etching Club. W. Gale had a studio in Lang-

ham Chambers at the time, and it was here, after
many meetings and many discussions, that the
Club was formed and became a fact.   Among the
members at the beginning were Millais, J. R.
Clayton, and several "Langhamites," including J.
Clark, H. Moore, Charles Keene, Smallfield, and
others.   The men used to meet at Lewis's chambers in Jermyn Street.   Here Whistler joined us,
and here I first saw him, not long returned from
Paris, and he told us many amusing anecdotes of his
experiences there, with stories of Ingres and other
painters.   Many pleasant hours were spent here
comparing proofs of our plates, in art discussions,
and etching "shop" talk.   After some time we were
emboldened to try the effect of a volume of our
united work with the public, and after much inter-
viewing and arrangements with publishers, which
part of the work was chiefly undertaken by Lewis,
we found one in the person of Mr. E. Gambart, the
great picture-dealer, and a volume of "Hood's
Poems, illustrated by the Junior Etching Club : E.
Gambart & Co., 25 Berners Street, 1858," was
presented to the world.   A second volume, "Passages from Modern English Poets," was published
in the following year by Day & Son.   This was
better in point of artistic merit than the first.   It
contained a very delicate etching by H. Moore
of a hen and chickens ; a characteristic Keene of

Pepys hurrying through a London street during the plague ; a good Millais ; specimens of J. Clark, and of Tenniel and Powell, now Sir John and Sir Francis, two of the last " birthday knights." So far as I remember, neither undertaking was a success in a pecuniary point of view, though we at least paid expenses and avoided debt. After this second venture· the Club gradually died ; the productions of the members may exist in the cabinets of the curious, and the titles of the two volumes occur occasionally in stray bookseller's catalogues.

The meetings of etchers were succeeded by meetings of singers. On Saturday evenings during the winter months a number of amateurs under the direction of John Foster, alto-singer in the choir of Westminster Abbey, sang part songs, glees, and madrigals.

The choir went by the name of the " Jermyn Band," from the name of the street in which the giver of the entertainments lived. Among the singers were the host himself ; Thomas W. Angell, who organised the post-office in the Crimea during the Russian war ; C. Keene, C. E. Perugini, Stanley Lucas, and Dr. Lavis. These evenings were a great success, crowded by notabilities, and as enjoyable as any evenings I ever remember. Smoking was indulged in *ad libitum*, as one's eyes, hair, and clothes testified next day. About eleven

o'clock the serious part of the concert was over
and a lavish feast of oysters having been satisfac-

AT ARTHUR LEWIS'S.

torily accounted for, Terpsichore gave place to
Thalia, and humorous songs or recitations filled up

the interval till "the chimes at midnight" gave the signal for departure.

PREACHING A SERMON AT MORAY LODGE.

In one of these post-prandial hours, Dr. Lavis sang a good-humoured skit of his own composition on the assembled company, their ways and peculiari-

ties, in which the present writer came in for a verse,
which I have remembered and give here, merely
premising that the " sermon " alluded to was a caricature of a camp-meeting oration which I occasionally preached (by desire) from the text, " For they
shall gnaw a file and flee into the mountains of
Hepsidam, where the lion roareth and the Wang-
doodle mourneth for his first-born."

The verse alluded to ran thus :

> " That wonderful sermon I fancy,
> Will live in our memories long,
> With poor ' Mrs. Waring ' and ' Nancy,'
> And that famous Pre-Raphaelite song.
> Of that school Marks his horror discloses,
> Yet paints, we are all well aware,
> Mediæval old cocks with red noses,
> But objects to young girls with red hair."

Of that Pre-Raphaelite song I preserved no
copy, and a memory, however retentive, will not
last for ever. It is as well perhaps to forget it,
for though written in perfect good-nature, it might
offend some who are slow to see humour when
connected with personality, however delicate that
personality may be. Some of my own relatives
are singularly deficient in this respect. I will,
therefore, only give those lines to which Dr. Lavis
more particularly referred :

"Well, yes, I am a P.R.B., one of the chosen clique,
    With high and pure imaginings, and some amount of
        cheek.'
I'm painting now a subject, 'Dante taken ill at night,'
Which great authority declares is 'exquisitely right,'
    And worth three other works of art all of the present
        time.*

"No vulgar daily life for me—for 'heart-work' I go in,
    Pare off the angle of the jaw and stick out well the
        chin,
    Give to bodies colic twistings—to eyes a dreamy stare,
    But that which most delights me is a woman with
        red hair.
    Which cheers the young Pre-Raphaelite all of the
    present time.

    (*Spoken*) She must have *red* hair."

Sometime in the early sixties, Arthur Lewis moved from Jermyn Street to a large and commodious house, Moray Lodge, Campden Hill, Kensington. The musical evenings were continued, and the singers were now known as "The Moray Minstrels." The concerts were given in the large billiard-room, the walls of which were decorated with trophies of arms, and coloured versions of sporting subjects by Leech which had appeared in *Punch* as plain woodcuts. The

* Mr. Ruskin, who wrote that a picture by Rossetti, Millais, or Holman Hunt was of more value than three pictures by any other painter.

billiard-table, its surface duly protected by a substantial cover, held stores of pipes, cigars, jars

44 MADDOX STREET W·

MINSTRELS

MORAY SMOKING

THE CONCERT

SEASON 1871

To

INVITATION CARD OF THE MORAY MINSTRELS.
Drawn by Frederick Walker.

of tobacco, and tankards and bottles of liquid
refreshments.   Smoking was unlimited, and the

atmosphere gradually became thick and of a de-
cidedly blue tone.   Many men of mark were to
be seen at those pleasant genial musters, though
painters predominated.   Three successive editors
of *Punch* have I seen there, Mark Lemon, Tom
Taylor, and F. C. Burnand.   The artistic staff
was well represented by John Leech, with his
sensitive and serious face, by the evergreen John
Tenniel, by Keene, Du Maurier, and Linley
Sambourne.   Among the painters, one caught an
occasional glimpse of Millais.   John Philip was
a frequent visitor, his face and figure reminding
one of his favourite Velasquez ; Frith, Egg, and
Elmore ; Ansdell, the animal painter ; Field Tal-
fourd, brother of the judge ; Harold Power, and
needless almost to add, each member of the St.
John's Wood Clique.   I have mentioned but a
tithe of the *habitués*, but there is one whose name
I must not omit to mention—Fred Walker—"altho'
the last, not least in our dear love."   He it was
who designed the cards of invitation for Lewis's
"At homes" for three years in succession.

The first drawing was of two female figures,
typical of "Music" and "Oysters," lifting a curtain
to reveal the "Morays" singing.   In another,
Minerva caresses her owl, while Apollo ceases for
a moment to twang his lyre as he lights his pipe.
A third represented a Bacchanalian dance in the

style somewhat of the decoration of Etruscan ware. This last was made for the season of 1867, which was the final year of the Saturday concerts at Moray Lodge, though the minstrels sang subsequently at Maddox Street and elsewhere. Arthur Lewis married Miss Kate Terry, and some of the most enjoyable evenings known in London came to a close, much to the regret of his numerous friends.

It was in the month of May 1864, when feeling that a change was necessary after the feverish excitement caused by finishing one's Academy work and the opening of the Exhibition, that G. D. Leslie and I went on a sketching expedition to Ewelme, an Oxfordshire village with a very picturesque combination of a church and wooden-cloistered almshouses. In the church there is a handsome monument to the grand-daughter of Chaucer, who founded the almshouses. A delightful brook, having its source in one of the principal gardens of the adjoining village, runs pleasantly by the side of the lane, about three miles in length, which connects Ewelme with Bensington, or Benson, as it is called, passing under numerous small tunnels and bridges, now developing into a sheepwash—now into a watercress bed—expanding into a mill-pond at Benson, and finally discharging itself into the Thames above Benson Weirs. There being but little accommoda-

tion at Ewelme, we put up at the Crown Inn,
Benson, the garden of which abutted on this same
mill-pond, of which more anon.   We took our meals
and slept only at the Crown, passing the working
days at Ewelme.   The weather was gloriously sunny,
the trees laden with blossoms, birds in full song,
while that tedious harbinger of east wind and other

The Arrival at Benson. MAY 14 1865

delights of an English May, the cuckoo, uttered
his exasperatingly monotonous note with "damn-
able iteration" from dawn to dusk.   But a little
distance from Ewelme was the sheepwash already
mentioned.   We stopped to watch the process of
washing whenever it took place.   A long space
of the brook was enclosed in compartments, the

bottom of which was dug out to different levels. In the highest and driest of these the patient fools waited to be washed.   In the deepest and most central division there were two trunks of trees, which had been hollowed out, in which the men engaged were protected up to their chests from the splashings caused by the washing and struggling of the sheep, who were only too glad to wade to the more shallow compartment.   Here huddled shiveringly together, they bleated their satisfaction that the bath was ended.   This was all so new and strange to the Cockney long "in populous city pent," that he may be pardoned for the description.

The almshouses and their occupants were our greatest attraction.   We liked the old people, and they took kindly to us, ever ready to offer the loan of a chair or any useful object their humble rooms afforded.   One old man was a great lover and keeper of bees; Tidmarsh was his name.   He was an old man-of-war's man, and had served as a boy in the battle of the Nile, and later in the action between the *Shannon* and the *Chesapeake*. Like another Andrew Fairservice, he would sit in front of his beehives in the almshouse garden with a book or newspaper, but his eye would ever and anon steal a watchful glance at the "skeps" to see how the bees were doing.   The hives were the old-fashioned basket ones, covered with large red

earthenware dishes—a quaint-looking arrangement.
I don't know whether Tidmarsh ever heard of "the
humane or non-depriving system by which we
never kill a bee;" but he was certainly a most
humane bee-master, for he never smoked out a hive,
or acted in any way aggressively to his insects, who
really appeared to return his consideration. When
a swarm was about taking place, though he would
warn us to keep out of the way, he moved among
the buzzing throng with perfect indifference; and
the queen once settled, would shake the swarm
into a fresh skep without the precaution of gloves
or veil. We saw him do this more than once,
whether the swarm had settled on a currant-bush,
or had, by mounting to a high branch of a tree,
rendered the use of a ladder necessary for its recovery. In the evenings at Benson we either strolled
about the inn-garden smoking the after-dinner pipe
or sketched some of the village children, who would
assemble round our sitting-room window during the
meal crying out in chorus, "Please, zur, will you
dra-a-w me to-night?" Once, not feeling inclined for
further work, we were loitering on the bank of the
mill-pond, enjoying the sweet evening air, when I
had a memorable encounter with a swan. A pair of
these birds had built their nest on a small island,
and the male, indignant at what he evidently considered an intrusion on his territory, would sail

close up to the pathway where we stood, his head
thrown back, his wings erect, while all his feathers,
ruffled up in rage, seemed to swell him to almost

EWELME CHILDREN.

double his normal size. This was his constant
practice whenever he saw us coming ; but now, for
some reason or another, he was more than ordinarily angry, and seeing me approach a little in

advance of Leslie, flew completely out of the water, dashing bodily at me. So sudden and unexpected was the attack, there was no chance of retreat. Instinctively I grasped the outstretched neck just below the head, but the weight of the bird and the impetus gained in his rapid flight were not to be resisted, and, still clinging to his throat, I toppled backwards, dragging the swan with me into a half-dry ditch which separated the pathway by the mill-pond from the garden. As soon as I scrambled out, which I did pretty quickly, my first thought was whether I had throttled the swan, my second whether he had injured me. The warmth of my hand and tightness of grasp had removed so much of the neck's soft down as to give the appearance of a feathered glove. I remembered gruesome stories of injuries that had been inflicted by a blow from the wing of an infuriated swan. Only the day before the miller's man told us he had been cutting rushes on the bank when the same swan struck him on the back with such force that he felt the effects of the blow for some days afterwards. But I was none the worse, save for the wetting and dirtying of my clothes. The swan, though sulky and discomfited, showed but very slight traces of the struggle. Leslie and I then helped him along by means of clothes props to a part where the bank was shelving, when he pulled himself together, and got again into the water, to our mutual content. I have ever since carefully avoided swans who, like Hecate, "look angrily."

We visited Ewelme again in the spring of the two following years, but did little on the last occasion. A hard unclouded blue sky accompanied by a searching east wind are not favourable conditions for English landscape, nor indeed for any. Detail seems multiplied and breadth destroyed when all is glare, grit, and glitter, and an evening sky without clouds is characterless and entirely devoid of charm. Nearly twenty years afterwards, when staying a few days with Leslie at his house on the river at Wallingford, we rowed to Benson and walked along the well-remembered lane to Ewelme. It was rather a melancholy visit. The church and almshouses were the same, but the old people, including the bee-keeper, had gone the way of all flesh. The village shops were losing their primitive character and aping those of the towns; plate-glass was supplanting the simple small-paned windows; advertisements of pills and soaps vulgarised the place, and the picturesque was vanishing before the march of modernisation. And there may have been feelings in one breast, at least, that all had not been done in that twenty years that might have been achieved, that certain aspirations remained still unfulfilled. But why pursue so painful

a subject? Many sketching expeditions did Leslie
and I have together. Once in company with J. E.
Hodgson we were at Pulborough, but the weather
was against us.* We had scarcely begun work one
morning when we were surprised by a fall of snow.
It was in the genial month of May. It was no

Gone forth to Work

good contending with the elements, so we went
to see an old mansion in the neighbourhood—

* I used to practise sketching during the annual holiday my wife
and family took with me. On one of these occasions we went to
Great Marlow, where I learned to row, and frequently diverted myself
of an evening in the very questionable manner shown in the illustration with a small revolver pistol which had been given me by a friend.
All I can say in palliation of my cruel intentions is, that this happened
thirty years ago. It is almost needless to say that I never even
maimed a swallow.

MARLOW

WAITING FOR A SHOT (in vain).

GREAT MARLOW.

Parham I think was its name. Returning in the
afternoon, we met a horseman galloping at a great
pace, bending down in his saddle and holding on
his hat, for the wind was keen and strong. "That
man's carrying the news of the Derby," said Hodgson. "Who's won?" we shouted as he came
within hearing. "Harmit!" shouted he in return
as he spurred his horse, and sweeping by like a
whirlwind quickly disappeared down the green
lanes. This is the only Derby day of which I,
degenerate and unsportsmanlike creature, can give
the date of my own knowledge—1867, or Her-
mit's year.

CHAPTER XII

IN the summer of 1859, in company with E. W. Russell, of whom mention has before been made, I went to Halifax to decorate part of a church which Mr. Edward Akroyd was building regardless of cost, and which he presented to the town. Sir Gilbert Scott was the architect, the sculpture and carvings were by John Philip, and Clayton & Bell executed the stained glass and designed the mural decorations. Russell and I were to be the executants, under their superintendence, of the twenty-four Elders and the Lamb over the chancel arch, and a number of angels with musical instruments on the panelled roof of the choir. On entering the church (dedicated, by the way, to All Souls), we found confusion worse confounded—masons, carvers, carpenters hard at work, and the air resounded with the numerous noises attendant on building. A broad solid scaffold had been erected for our use by the wall of the chancel, some fifty feet at least from the ground. Ascending the ladder to reach this bad eminence, we felt nervous and giddy on getting to the top, not daring to stand upright, even far from the edge, but feeling more inclined to grovel on all fours. Fortunately the designs had not arrived. We employed the interval in getting accustomed to the dizzy height and smoking many pipes. This nervous feeling, however, soon disappeared, giving place to an indifference that would allow us to stand on the verge of the platform and remove our overalls as we stood on one leg. We used to dine at mid-day at an ordinary held at a neighbouring tavern, frequented chiefly by commercials, and gigantic farmers on market-days, men with appetites of wonderful enormity. Their behaviour at table was eccentric rather than nice. They dipped their knives into the gravy of the dish before them, returned them to their capacious lips, and having sucked them dry, would dip the implements again and again, without the performance exciting any remark.

Returning to the church after dinner one day, we were about to mount our ladder, when we were aware of a small curate, attached or about to be attached to the edifice. Wishing to do the civil thing by him, we invited him to sup with us one night at our lodgings. " I shall be very glad," said he, "for I cordially approve of this mingling of class with class!" Our friend imagined from our holland suits that we were house-painters. During our simple supper, Russell innocently intimated that he had a brother then studying at Oxford, which information, though it didn't surprise the cleric to any extent, yet made him "sit up" all the same!

For more than two months we were engaged on these decorative paintings. On the fine Sundays we took walks and penetrated the surrounding country. One was devoted to a pilgrimage to Haworth, celebrated as the home of the Brontës. We reached there in time for afternoon service, and heard the Rev. Mr. Brontë—a white-headed, sad, and somewhat stern-faced old gentleman—preach. At the reading-desk below him sat the Rev. Mr. Nicholls, his curate, and husband of Charlotte Brontë, who died but a year after her marriage, and four years before our visit. We saw the monument to her memory in one of the aisles of the church. The home of the Brontës stood, and may now stand, close by. An old housekeeper was walking in the garden, who plucked and gave us some flowers as remem-

August 8th 1859

HALIFAX—DECORATING THE CHANCEL ROOF.

brances, and pointed out the window of the room in which Charlotte was accustomed to write. It was now time to start on our way back if we would reach Halifax before dark, which we did with no adventure by the way beyond nearly losing our way on a desolate moor, and having a little difficulty in a bog, of which we were unaware.

The next day at our ordinary it was difficult to make the Yorkshire giants believe that we had walked to Haworth, and not only walked there, but back. It struck them, who never thought of walking if they could ride, as something extraordinary that the feat of covering about fourteen miles on foot should have been performed by two men who were so far below their standard of size and stature—by men who were Cockneys, moreover.

While in Halifax we made some acquaintances living a little way out of the town, who asked us to partake of their Sunday hospitality. Hospitality indeed! After this lapse of time, I recall it shudderingly. A very substantial dinner in the middle of the day had scarcely been swallowed before the table was spread again for an equally substantial and heavy tea, at which, if we did not gorge ourselves beyond repletion, our hosts, more especially the hostess, would feel aggrieved and hurt. Huge hams, prodigious joints, eggs boiled or poached, with tea-cakes hot and buttered, washed down with copious draughts of tea, ensured present distension and future indigestion.   After an entertainment of this kind it was difficult to waddle rather than walk, like turkeys crammed for Christmas, to the railway station !

I was employed in church decoration for Clayton & Bell the following year, this time alone.   It was at a place called Salter Hebble, not far from Halifax.   The chancel arch was again the field to be covered, but though I noted the fact, I failed to record the subject, nor can I now recollect what it was.   An incident impressed itself on my memory which I will relate.   One evening after work, I was making some pencil notes of a rugged bit of landscape in the neighbourhood of some cotton-mills.   The mill-hands were coming out, and seeing me with sketch-book and pencil looking in their direction, concluded, or pretended to conclude, I was an objectionable overseer.   "He be takin' thy time, lad," was the cry.   The boys of the party shied stones at me with such precision and rapidity, that remembering the old proverb on valour and discretion, and failing to appreciate the humour of the playful Yorkshire rough, I thought it best to beat a retreat.

After the church the theatre.   The frieze over the proscenium of the Gaiety Theatre (Mr. C. J. Phipps, architect) was designed and executed by

A . Suburban Street . Halifax . Aug.t 7. 59.

A WET SUNDAY MORNING.

me in 1868. J. B. Burgess being away in Spain, was good enough to lend me his studio in Maida Vale in which to paint it. The canvas was over thirty feet long, and hinged in the centre; there was not space enough to straighten it, so it had to be cut in halves. By a lucky fluke, it so happened that I had designed the drawing in such a way that this division did not interfere with the work as a whole. Everything connected with the building and decoration of a theatre has to be done in a hurry. I began at once, enlarged the drawing on to the canvas, and by working hard, got it finished in six weeks and sent it to the theatre eleven days before the opening. I saw it for the first time complete and *in situ* on the Sunday a week before that event occurred. The walls of the theatre were streaming with wet, every gas jet was alight, turned on to the full, and large braziers of burning coke increased the condensation by the heat they emitted. No wonder that I caught a violent cold which prevented my being present on the opening night. The upper part of a proscenium is an absurd place for a decoration; nobody can see it properly but the "gods," and they don't care to look at it. The hot mephitic air from the gas and other causes, increasing in foulness as it rises upwards, must blacken and gradually obliterate the

simplest and most solid painting. Mr. Hollingshead, then manager of the Gaiety, often expressed
to me, half laughingly, a wish that the proprietor
would remove the painting and give him a clock
in its place. It is some time since I was at this
theatre, but those who have tried to see it tell
me that the decoration is all but invisible. I may
therefore be allowed to mention that the subject
is a masque or dance being performed before a
mediæval king and queen with their court. The
original sketch is in the possession of Mr. Armi-
tage, R.A., who thought well enough of it to buy
it from me.

Another proscenium frieze of my design and
painting (1879) is—for I have not yet heard of
the theatre being burnt down—that of the Theatre
Royal, Manchester. "Shakespeare enthroned between Tragedy and Comedy," and surrounded by
many of the chief characters of his plays, is the
subject. It was painted in Elgin Road, Maida
Vale, in the rooms formerly occupied by Leslie.
When placed in the theatre it was cemented to the
wall, and thus kept flat and unwrinkled. At the
Gaiety, the old-fashioned stretcher was employed,
which naturally conduced to warping and other
vagaries with the changes of temperature. The first
night of the "Royal" was in October 1879, when
"As You Like It" was performed. Mr. Calvert was

the manager (since dead), and Mr. A. Darbyshire the architect of the theatre, or of the alterations and additions thereof.

Many may or may not have noticed a decorative frieze running along the outside of the Albert Hall at South Kensington. It is high on the wall, so close to the roof as not to unnecessarily inconvenience the passer-by by obliging him to look at it. The whole is executed in mosaic of terra-cotta. The first completed portion of this was enlarged from my drawings, comprised Agriculture, Astronomy, Shipbuilding, and Navigation, and may be descried from the Horticultural Gardens. Merely noting that in one of the galleries at South Kensington Museum there is a lunette of "Anatomy" painted by the writer, we will pass from public to private buildings.

My picture of "The Bookworm," exhibited at the Academy in 1871, was painted for the library at Crewe Hall, and formed a panel over the mantle-piece—it is less decorative than pictorial. Lord Crewe had previously given me a commission for six panels of the "Virtues"—Truth, Temperance, Humility, &c. (sarcastic friends naturally remarked that the "Vices" would be more in my line). These were nearly life-size figures on arched-top panels, with incised gold background. For Birket Foster's summer-house at Witley I painted a series of

Shakespeare's Seven Ages,* on panels with gold backgrounds.   Scenes from the works of the same poet furnished subjects to fill circular spaces in the ceiling of the billiard-room of the Rev. Mr. Bridges at Beddington House, Croydon.   I did a good length of English rustic subjects for Mr. Stewart Hodgson's house at Lythe Hill, Haslemere —haymaking, driving home the cows, ploughing, angling, &c., and later on four large lunettes of birds, flamingoes, pelicans, storks, and cranes, for the staircase of his mansion in South Audley Street. Other bird subjects were executed for Mr. H. Hucks Gibb's drawing-room in his place at Elstree. For my friend R. W. Edis's dining-room in Fitzroy Square I painted figures of Fish, Flesh, Fowl, Wine, Beer, and Tobacco — the banquet, arrival and departure of the guests.   In the front drawing-room are fanciful garden scenes with female figures. In the room beyond, conventional birds disport themselves.   Four large canvases of the " Seasons " were painted for Mr. T. Vaughan of Gunnergate Hall, near Middlesbrough.   The first of these, " Winter," was in the Royal Academy Exhibition of 1874.   But I will not exhaust the reader's patience

---

* These panels were sold at Christie's in April of this year, and knocked down for a very modest sum.   I am glad to think they have found a congenial home, where they have been appropriately framed and are carefully looked after.   Mr. S. B. Bancroft bought them himself in Christie's rooms.

28 nov 1877

TOWNSHEND HOUSE,
NORTH GATE,
REGENTS PARK. N.W.

my dear Marks

Simply Bachelors. ?
Tuesday 7. p. m.

Spring.

FIRST SKETCH FOR DECORATIVE PICTURE PAINTED FOR THE BILLIARD-ROOM AT GUNNERSGATE HALL.

Billiards.

further with this dry catalogue beyond mentioning two small panels for the entrance-hall of Alma Tadema's house, for which he munificently overpaid me by an exquisite little half-length portrait of my eldest daughter. Reserving for the present any remarks on painted furniture, I proceed to describe the most important wall decoration I have ever done.

It was, I think, at the private view of the R.A. in 1874 that I was introduced to the Duke of Westminster by Alfred Waterhouse, who was then rebuilding and altering the hall at Eaton, Chester. Our conversation took place near the deco-

STUDIES FOR A FIGURE IN A PANEL PAINTED FOR ALMA TADEMA.

rative picture of "Winter" hung in the lecture-
room, which was not then the sculpture gallery it is
now.   After asking what other decorative work I had

Summer.

Autumn.

done, his Grace expressed a wish that I should do
some work for Eaton—a wish to which I was only
too willing to accede, and it was arranged I should

go to Eaton in a few days to see the spaces to be filled. At the end of May I went down, arriving shortly before the dinner-hour. The Duke was riding, but ready to meet me by the time I had dressed. We had a *tête-à-tête* dinner in some small room which was not invaded by carpenters and masons. My host's manner was grave but kindly

Winter.

and courteous. Our meal finished, he said, " Now smoke ; all my friends do." I hesitated, knowing he was no smoker, and murmured something about not being a slave to the habit ; but the Duke saw through this feebly urged excuse, and said with a smile, " Now light up." I did not require to be told twice. We then chatted away pleasantly on various

topics, but chiefly, of course, on the subject of the
future decoration, for which I suggested Chaucer's
Canterbury Pilgrims, as affording good opportunity
for variety of character in man and horse, and as
being in harmony with the style of the architecture.
It was now, although early, time to retire for the
night.   The Duke, taking one chamber candlestick,
and handing me another, preceded me to the saloon,
a large and lofty apartment, adjoining the entrance-
hall from which it was entered by a tall archway.
This occupies one end of the saloon, while the
other is filled by windows, leaving two long side
walls for the surface to be decorated.   All was
litter and confusion of carpenter's benches, planks,
trestles, &c.   Lit only by two small candles, the
vast room seemed to be of Brobdingnagian proportions.   My heart all but sank within me as I
said, " Do I understand your Grace intrusts both
these walls to me ? "   " Certainly," replied the Duke.
Then we went upstairs.   I followed, feeling like
a guilty wretch on his way to the scaffold.   He
left me at the door of my bedroom, shook hands
and said " good-night."   I went to bed, but not to
sleep.   I was too excited, thinking of the magni-
tude of the task I had undertaken.   My room,
moreover, was near the stables, or at least in
close proximity to some outside clock, which
chimed not the hours only, but the quarters.

How I blessed that clock as I made many in-
effectual efforts to drop off between the hour and
the quarter past—the half-hour and the quarter
to. It was not so much the actual chiming, but
knowing that another would sound in a few
minutes, that tended to "murder sleep." But un-
consciousness came at last, and I awoke refreshed
and hearty, and with my nervousness considerably abated. I returned to town at once, but it
was not till the end of the year—for there was
no hurry—that I made the designs for the Canterbury Pilgrims in water-colours. The Duke
came to see them, expressed his approval, and
carried them off in a hansom-cab to show to
the Duchess. They were exhibited at the Royal
Academy in 1875. As it would be months, even
years, before the saloon would be sufficiently advanced to receive the decorations, the first was
not begun before May 1876. Both were painted
on canvases over thirty-five feet long, and as my
studio was not sufficiently spacious to accommodate
such large surfaces on the usual stretchers, I con-
sulted with John O'Connor, then scene-painter at
the Haymarket Theatre. By his direction, the
stage-carpenter, a very ingenious fellow named
Wales, rigged up two upright poles securely and
strongly attached to the studio wall. On these
the canvas was strained like a scroll, so that

when part of about ten feet in length was finished,
it could be rolled up, and an equal length of bare
canvas displayed ready for the painter's work.
Each picture when finished was rolled, carefully
packed in a strong deal box, and sent to Grosvenor
House, till such time as it was required at Eaton.
Both were finished in April 1878, but it was
exactly four years later when I saw them in the
hall and worked on them.   There was little to be
done beyond touching up the sky here and there
and putting in a few clouds.

Meanwhile, I had received from and executed
for the Duke another commission.   It was one
the carrying out of which gave me more pleasure
and enjoyment than any that I ever had.   In
November 1877 I was painting some tiny panels of
heads of birds for my old fellow-student William
Burges.   The Duke happened to call to see how
the "Pilgrims" were progressing, and seemed very
interested with these birds' heads, looking at them
again and again.   At length he said, "How would
a room of birds look?"   I replied, I thought it
would have a very decorative effect, when he gave
me to understand I might carry out his idea.
When next I was at Eaton, the Duke, Waterhouse, and I went over the hall together, selected
a room (one of the smaller drawing-rooms), and
decided on the number (twelve) and position of

the panels. It was arranged that these should be in groups of three. As I wished to include birds of all shapes and sizes, of different climes and conditions, from the Indian adjutant to the humble English wagtail, the cockatoo from Australia, the macaw from South America, the African crane, and the European stork, I imagined them in a fairy garden, an ornithological Walhalla, where no bird quarrels with another, but is content with the climate, conditions, and surroundings of its present abode—an abode where food is always present without the trouble of seeking for it, into which bands of yelling school-children are not permitted to enter, those terrors of the actual "Zoo;" where pinioning is forbidden, and wing-hacking unknown.

Before the birds settled down in their permanent home at Eaton, they were exhibited at Agnew's Gallery in Bond Street in May 1880. The little show brought me kind and congratulatory letters (among others) from the President, Sir J. E. Millais, and Briton Rivière, and had the honour of supplying the text for a leader in the *Times*.

Never has any work of mine been so well cared for or shown to such advantage. The frames of the pictures are richly carved and gilt; the walls covered with a warm but delicately tinted grey plush or velvet, which relieves the darks and gives value to the lights of the painting. I believe Miss

Centre.

Jabiru

Night Heron.

A.S.M.

ONE OF TWELVE PANELS PAINTED FOR THE DRAWING-ROOM AT EATON.

Jekyll of Henley-on-Thames is the lady to whom I am indebted for this arrangement.

Let me add that I have never worked for any one so kindly considerate and sympathetic as I found the Duke of Westminster.

About the year 1860 I decorated some furniture for W. Burges, the architect, or rather artist-architect, for he could design a chalice as well as a cathedral, and draw with his own hand all the necessary details. He was a learned archæologist. His favourite period was the thirteenth century, while the style he disliked almost to hatred was that called Queen Anne. It is not as an architect, however, that I have to speak of him, but as a decorator. When I first met Burges, it was at Leigh's in Newman Street, where he then happened to be engaged on a "diaper" of rampant lions, though he drew from the "antique" or the life usually. We entered into conversation. I found we had many tastes in common, and a few days afterwards I found myself in his chambers, No. 15 Buckingham Street, overlooking the river, a house which, according to rumour, Peter the Great once lived in.

The walls of the room in which I found Burges were painted in distemper with conventional draperies, and trees above, on which were perched birds such as were never seen by mortal eye, drawn either by Burges or by any friend who happened to look in. These were done in outline filled in with a flat tint. In the centre of the room was a lofty cabinet for books on art, the doors divided out in a painted architectural arrangement of pillars and arches, the whole crowned with parapet and gables. The panels were arranged to have a figure composition in each, by young painters, adherents to the Gothic revival movement, of subjects from Pagan and Christian history. Burne Jones, Albert Moore, Poynter, Smallfield, and others, had already contributed their work. The rectangular base had merely the ground laid for the decorations; these I painted under Burges's superintendence and from his suggestion—a concert of the Pierides, half women, half birds, occupying the two centre panels flanked by single figures of Arachne and Syrinx.

Another piece of furniture was a mediæval settle; on the back of this were three panels of burnished gold, which I found rather glaring when painting on them. The central subject was Sol enthroned watching the signs of the Zodiac dancing a break-down. Leo is flirting with Virgo; Cancer, the Gemini, Taurus, Aries, Libra, and Scorpio, Sagittarius, and Capricornus all vie in footing it featly, while Aquarius as a pump is inducing the Pisces to take the Temperance pledge. The ideas in this composition were Burges's own. So also with two figures I painted

for his chest of drawers—"Clean Clothes," an
Oxford man in fresh flannels, and "Dirty Clothes,"
a modern navvy with clay-stained smock; the notions
emanated from the same playful fancy. A series
of small heads of birds for the inside panels of a
bookcase already referred to was the only work I did
for him without being "coached." He liked articles
of furniture generally to suggest or symbolise their
contents. Two instances may be given of this, which
are combined with his irrepressible love of fun—a
bookcase painted by F. Weekes with figures all connected with architecture and alphabetically arranged.
A. was an architect—Burges himself with a huge
pair of compasses, at work; B. was a builder with
a great bill, &c.; and a wardrobe with represen-
tations of "Flax," a young girl with her distaff;
"Wool," a piping shepherd surrounded by his sheep
—while the joke came in below with a procession
of shears and other implements of the tailor.

I speak under correction, but believe Burges
was the first architect in this century to revive the
art of painting furniture. It was not alone in
that or in architecture that his fertility and fancy
in design were displayed. He had an extraordinary talent as a designer of goldsmith's work.
His decanters, cups, jugs, forks, and spoons were
designed with an equal ability to that with which
he would design a castle or a cathedral. No man

enjoyed his work more than he, or felt a more
childish joy in designing and seeing that design
carried out.   There is a nursery rhyme I have
heard Burges himself recite which epitomises his
character.   The author was Dante Rossetti—

> " An architect named William Burges,
>   From childhood scarcely emerges ;
>   If you had not been told
>   He's disgracefully old,
>   You would offer some bull's-eyes to Burges ! "

It had long been Burges's ambition to build himself a house of his own, in which he could indulge
in his fads and quaint conceits, and gratify to the
full his taste for the beautiful to his heart's content.
I am aware the word "beautiful" may seem wrongly
applied in the present case.   Burges's ideas of
beauty may not be those of Brown or of Robinson,
but are they therefore to be deprecated?   Burges
got a site for his house in Melbury Road, but
did not live to finish it.   I saw less of him after
he left Buckingham Street, but I shall always think
of him as a man of most consistent cheerfulness,
as a buoyant, happy creature.   Other men have
their moments of depression—Burges seemingly
never.   He was a studious antiquary, and had
read much ; the stores of information he possessed
he was always ready to impart liberally and with-

out ostentation.   He never, in the slang of the
hour, put "side" on.

He was elected A.R.A. in January 1881, but
did not live long enough to enjoy the humours
of the varnishing days, or take his seat at the
Academy banquet in the following May.   He died
after a brief illness, and was buried at Norwood
Cemetery.

FIRST SKETCH FOR PART OF THE ALBERT HALL FRIEZE.

CHAPTER XIII

I N comparing the R.A. students of my time with those I met at Paris, the difference between them was not so very strongly marked. Both were equally noisy and prone to skylarking.

The English had not that proverbial mixture of the tiger and the monkey, but the occasional cruelty was, I am willing to believe, nearly always owing to thoughtlessness in the French students ; and, as I have elsewhere stated, their treatment of me as a foreigner afforded me little cause for complaint.

The average R.A. student of forty years ago was rougher in manner, poorer in pocket, and of humbler social status than he of to-day. The admission of women to the schools has undoubtedly done much to refine and civilise him. For instance, quarrels ending in stand-up fights would not unfrequently take place; the students were left entirely without control or supervision during the absence of the keeper from the antique school for hours at a stretch. A curator was appointed in my time, Mr. Woodington, who never left the school during working hours, and was held responsible for peace and order. This at once made a change for the better. But on the evening when medals and prizes were awarded, in the interval between the students taking their places in the lecture-room and the filing in of the Academicians with the President at their head, the fun and noise were fast and furious, and, unawed by the presence of " the forty," the students' behaviour was so contumacious that they did not hesitate to express disapprobation if the honours were not awarded to their satisfaction. A notable case of this kind occurred on the evening of December 10, 1857, the first time the Turner gold medal was given. Henry Moore was among the competitors, and, in the opinion of a large majority of the students, the one who would take the medal. So sure were we that Moore would come in an easy first, that we could hardly believe our ears when the name of the prize-winner was

read out, a name that was *not* Moore.   There was
dead silence for a moment or two, to be broken
by a storm of hisses from a malcontent and rebellious band.   Strange that the earth did not open
to swallow us up.   The Academy maintained its
dignity, and very wisely took no notice of conduct
so mutinous and reprehensible.   Events proved
that the judgment of the students was not so far out,
however questionably expressed.   " The whirligig
of time" brought its "revenges."   Henry Moore
was twenty-eight years later elected A.R.A., and
became R.A. in 1893.

The incident related above happened so long
ago as to be nearly forgotten.   I hope, therefore,
I may be forgiven for reproducing some lines
written at the time :—

EPIGRAM.

In grave debate the R.A.'s meet ;—
" Invention, feeling, we ignore.
Colour and nature—nonsense ! stuff !
For Heaven's sake let's have no Moore ! "

That the student was poorer and of humbler
social position in my time was evidenced partly
by the fact that not more than two or three, in the
antique school at least (I never got into the " Life "),
were possessed of a dress suit.   The medal-nights
were not the stately affairs they are now.   It was

not till the reign of Sir Francis Grant that the
members, even, at his suggestion, appeared in
evening-dress, to add to the dignity of the distribu-
tion. There were no ladies then to contribute grace
and colour to the ceremony; and as to the students
having a champagne-supper afterwards, to which
they invited the President and those members who
had served as visitors in the schools, such an
idea was never dreamt of, and would have made
some of the older Presidents turn in their graves!
The only suppers then were among the students
themselves at some neighbouring public or chop
house, where the meal was humble and inexpen-
sive, with steaks and porter in place of made
dishes and champagne.

I had not long been a student when I came to
know G. D. Leslie and G. A. Storey, who worked
of an evening at the Academy. John Brett also
studied there in the daytime. Before leaving this
part of my subject, I may refer to an incident
which recurs to memory in thinking of these days.
The public funeral of the Duke of Wellington
took place in November 1852, and any student who
wished was allowed to view the imposing procession from the top of the National Gallery, as it
wound its slow length along to place the body of
the hero of Waterloo by the side of the remains
of the hero of Trafalgar.

An election-night is always a great function at the Royal Academy, greater and with more attendant excitement for an A.R.A. than for a R.A., the latter being in many cases a certainty, while there is always uncertainty as to the result of an election of an Associate. Let me describe the process. From about half-past seven in the evening the members begin to arrive, each one signing his name as he enters in a book kept for that purpose, as a proof of attendance. Tea and coffee are provided, and the candidates' claims and chances discussed. In winter-time, elections are conducted in the lecture-room ; in one of the smaller galleries in the summer months. On the stroke of eight the President takes the chair, and the minutes of last meeting being read and confirmed, the secretary hands a printed list of the names of the candidates to every member, who at once makes a mark or "scratch" against one name only, and thereupon places it in a basket in front of the President. In former days these papers had to be signed by the member voting. If he omitted to do this, the vote was lost. The practice was given up years ago, and the papers are no longer signed. When every one has voted, the President rising, takes the papers one by one, and calls aloud the name scratched. These are noted down by the secretary and other officials. The last name having

been read out, the numbers are totted up. The
name of each candidate which has secured four
or more "scratches" is then written on a blackboard, thus—

> A ... ...
> B ... ...
> C ... ...
> D ... ...
> E ... ...

The printed lists are again distributed, and only
one of the names on the blackboard can be scratched
for. The lists are handed in, the names called out,
the numbers added as before, when the result of
the blackboard is found to be—

> A 15
> B 10
> C 14
> D 6
> E 10

A and C having the highest scores, are then
ballotted for in the usual way, the members coming
up to the table as their names are called by the
secretary from the book signed on entrance. Each
receives a cork ball from the President, and
deposits it in the ballot-box, to the right or left,
for either A or C. By this time the number
of members present is known, and whether the

President counts the balls in the winning or in the losing drawer first, the final result is divulged.   The name of the successful candidate is wafted from gallery to gallery, till it reaches the doors of the entrance-hall, where a group of "models" is sure to be waiting for the news, each one eager to be the first to get into a hansom and drive as quickly as possible to the house of the fortunate painter or sculptor with the glad tidings, to be rewarded by the customary "tip" of a sovereign.   Sometimes it happens that the first elected one lives at some distance from town, in which case there is much disappointment in the crowd of models, who relieve themselves with curses and gnashing of teeth! Architects do not employ professional models—at least, I never knew but one who did, and he is no longer here.   Imagine, therefore, the surprise of a most distinguished member of that profession when an oddly-dressed, half-breathless man invaded his drawing-room, proclaimed the news, and waited for the tip.   My friend not knowing the custom, explanations were made, when, more amused than annoyed, he gave the model his fee, who bowed himself out.   He had not got clear of the house, however, when another hansom was heard at the street door, and Model No. 2 came to try it on. The architect, though possessed of humour, thought the joke was becoming stale.   However, he gave the fellow his gratuity, and saw him off the premises. There was actually another model on the road, but the new Associate, fearing "the line would stretch out to the crack of doom," thought it time to strike, had the door barred, the gas turned down, and straightway regained the interrupted privacy of his sanctum.

I should have mentioned that in the event of two or more Associates being elected the same evening, the process described above has to observed in each case *de novo*. The election of an Academician is similar to that of an Associate, but there are no models in waiting, as the new R.A. knows of his own election the instant it has taken place.

On an Associate election-night, the Arts Club in Hanover Square is in a state of great excitement. Many members of the Royal Academy are also members of the "Arts;" indeed it has often been jokingly affirmed that, in order to be received into the Academic fold, it is necessary, as a preliminary measure, to belong to the Club. The first detachment from the Academy brings the news of "who's in," which is quickly spread by the waiters throughout the Club, the largest room of which is filled with an expectant crowd—

> "To hear our only Orator expound
> The hero's merit, and themselves to drain
> (At his expense) a bumper of champagne!"

"Our only Orator" is one of the earliest and best-known members of the "Arts," with ready flow of eloquence and an aptitude for humorous simile and allusion. He is to make a speech on the occasion, as he has done on twenty others, to propose the health of the new A.R.A.'s. Champagne is brought in in magnums, order called, glasses filled; the orator springs to his feet, and in a flow of remarkable eloquence renders homage to the power of the hero or heroes of the hour, wilfully exaggerating their artistic achievements. Rounds of laughter and applause greet him as he sits down, while the newly-elected rises to respond; and though "the words of Mercury are harsh after the songs of Apollo," the recipient of the honour says his few sentences with simplicity and modest manliness. The evening comes to an end, and those who have work on the morrow disperse to their homes in the draughty hansom, or closer and window-rattling four-wheeler.

I was not at the "Arts" at the time of my election as A.R.A., but at a friend's house, having given intimation to all whom it might concern where I was to be found. The model I employed mostly then, a would-be cynic, but so child-like and bland as to be easily gulled, was waiting in the doorway, when another, more wide-awake and enterprising, pushed inside the entrance,

and seeing my man, said, "Marks is not in; it's
Marcus Stone." The simpleton believed this, and
walked away disconsolate, while the other jumped
into a hansom and brought the news to St. John's
Wood. On the afternoon of that day I com-
mitted an act of rashness which friends afterwards described as a tempting of Providence.
From various sources, I had heard that my
"coming in" was all but assured. I wrote the
news to some relatives and friends—the news
which they would receive by first post next day.
The results of an election did not then, as now,
appear in the morning newspapers. Had I not
got in, the cards would have been destroyed and
my temerity never known. Three Associates were
admitted to the Academy on the evening of January
26, 1871, and the order of election was as follows :—
Henry Stacy Marks, Frederick Walker, Thomas
Woolner.

How it was that I was elected first, instead of
second or third, I have never been able to understand.

Some week or so after, we three were summoned
to the old building in Trafalgar Square, duly appearing in evening-dress. After waiting a short time,
we were ushered into the Council-chamber. The
light of lamps and candles was concentrated on
the green baize table; the faces of the President

and the ten councillors were relieved against the
deep gloom beyond the table. A pleasant sense
of cozy warmth pervaded the room. The secretary,
J. P. Knight, read the duties that were expected
of us; we then signed "the Instrument," with its
long roll of names, some illustrious, some forgotten,
and having shaken hands all round, departed. I got
my diploma in a few days, signed by the President
and the secretary. It is a full Academician's diploma
only that bears the autograph of Her Majesty.

Few pleasanter times can there be than those
technically called "varnishing days" at the Royal
Academy. The members all meet together after
months of separation and exchange their experiences
and accounts of their doings and travels during
the past twelve months. But, as in all mundane
pleasures, there is the usual note of sadness. These
days are milestones in life's road, reminding us
how age with stealing steps has clawed us in his
clutch, and of the friends and confreres who have
dropped out of the march and left sad gaps in
the ranks. It is rare for a year to pass without
at least one loss. In that in which I write, no
less than three have occurred—Woolner, Pettie,
and Vicat Cole. Pettie's death was felt the more
being so entirely unexpected. On the first varnishing day, or at least in the morning thereof, there
is gloom on the brow and a chill at the heart of

each member, caused by the shock of seeing his picture for the first time on the Academy walls. It looks so different there to what it did in the studio, in size, in aspect, in every way to what he had fondly thought it did in the studio under the most favourable light, no rival near it, and surrounded by adventitious aids to attract and allure the buyer.

But each member finds every one else equally down-hearted, so the morning wears on till the hour of luncheon approaches, when the thought of that substantial meal raises his spirits and calms his fears. The head-porter blows a whistle, the signal that lunch is ready ; a crowd of hungry men is assembled in the Water Colour gallery, and the President appearing, the door leading thence to the refreshment-room is unlocked, and the famished ones follow him to the regions below. Two toasts only are given at this entertainment, the health of the Queen, and that of those Associates who have been gathered to the Academy ranks since last we sat at that festive board. The fish-knives, forks, spoons, and other plate, are mostly the gifts of members, for when an A.R.A. develops into an R.A., it is usual, though not compulsory, to celebrate an event so interesting, to himself at least, by contributing some item to the store of Academic silver. One man of practical turn will give inkstands or candlesticks; another a tea or coffee pot, a beaker or tazza. Wishing to be associated with the more convivial moments of my colleagues, I presented a cigar and cigarette box of a richly grained wood inlaid with and mounted in silver, with the date of presentation and the royal arms engraved thereon. My friend J. R. Clayton designed this for me, but it was not complete without a motto—a motto it must have, and if possible, a Shakespearian one. Now, the difficulty was, that, as is well known, while Ben Jonson and most, if not all, of Shakespeare's contemporaries have continual references to tobacco and smoking, or "drinking" it, the bard never alludes to it. Was this owing, I wonder, to a courtier-like deference to James I. and the royal opinions so emphatically expressed in the famous "Counterblaste"? After some consideration I decided on the passionate exclamation of Othello to Desdemona—

" O thou weed,
Who art so lovely, fair, and smell'st so sweet!"

I felt as proud as a peacock when I had solved this problem, and as pleased as Punch.

Three Presidents of the Royal Academy have I known—Sir Charles Eastlake, Sir Francis Grant, and Sir Frederick Leighton. I was never introduced to Sir Charles, and remember only his grave,

courtly manner and pale melancholy face.   To Sir
Francis, on the other hand, I was introduced
several times, but vanished somehow from his
memory between each introduction.   A tall handsome man, of commanding presence, the type of an
English gentleman, with a genial pleasant manner
when you knew him, but, as the song says, you'd
got to know him first.   My first picture after I was
elected Associate was "The Bookworm," painted for
Lord Crewe.   At luncheon on the first varnishing
day, I heard Sir Francis say to Elmore, who sat
next him, "Who's that man in the red tie?"   When
the meal was concluded he came round to where I
was seated, warmly shook me by the hand, and
congratulated me on my work.   He never forgot
me after that, and was always kind and friendly.
He died in 1878, and a large number of members
went by train to Melton Mowbray for the funeral
on the 12th October.   The day was warm and
sunny, with a bright blue sky.   The Archbishop
of York, whose tall manly figure gained additional
dignity in his canonicals, read the service very
impressively.   No sooner had he begun by the
grave-side than a robin, perched on a branch immediately over the Archbishop's head, with his soft
liquid song made a touching accompaniment to the
deep tones of the prelate's voice as he read the
solemn words for the burial of the dead.

Some few of us went to the principal inn of the town for a smoke, to while away the time till our train was to start for London.   There were some farmers and sporting-looking characters in the room in which we sat, and all spoke of the deceased President with respect and affection.   " I saw him married," said one old fellow, " but I never thought I should live to see him buried."

Though not a good orator, the speeches of Sir F. Grant at the Academy banquets were distinguished by good sound sense.   Accustomed to mix in the best society, he had learned how to say the right thing in the right way with tact and courtesy, skilfully keeping clear of any remarks or opinions at which umbrage might be taken.

He was succeeded by Sir Frederick Leighton in 1868, and in December of the same year I had the honour of being the first Academician elected under the new presidency, in the place of Sir Francis.   I had already enjoyed the privilege of Sir Frederick's friendship long before he became President, before even he was A.R.A.   I first met him at the rooms in Jermyn Street, at one of the Arthur Lewis concerts.   Sir Frederick was then, in intervals snatched from painting, illustrating George Eliot's " Romola " as it appeared in the pages of the *Cornhill Magazine.*

Of him I will only say that it is difficult to

imagine a President more able, or one who could
with more devotion, energy, and conscientiousness
carry out the multifarious duties connected with his
office—duties which increase in number year by
year, if not month by month.   It would be imper-
tinent in me to enlarge further on his ability, but
I could not well have said less.

The annual dinner of the Royal Academy is a
brilliant and imposing spectacle not readily forgotten.   It takes place in the large room known
as Gallery No. III.   Preparations are made for a
little more than 250 diners.   A long table extend-
ing the whole length of the gallery has offshoots,
some eight in number, of shorter tables, placed at
right angles.   In the centre of this long board of
honour the presidential chair is placed, to the right
and left of which are seats for princes of the royal
blood, ambassadors, dignitaries of the Church, Her
Majesty's Ministers, &c.   At the other tables,
admirals, generals, judges, doctors, men eminent
in science and literature—in short, celebrities of all
kinds, find places with the Academicians and Associates.   A more magnificent dining-room could not
be found in London, nor one more worthy of such
a distinguished company.   The large masses of
white tablecloth, the beautiful flowers, the gold
and silver plate, relieved against the picture-covered
walls, make a unique and harmonious effect of

colour, for the full enjoyment of which daylight is necessary.   There is plenty of time for this, as the dinner is at an early hour, and the sun sets late.

The galleries are open at two o'clock, and many of the invited avail themselves of the opportunity to have a quiet look at the pictures before dressing for dinner.   Between five and six the rooms begin to fill. ˙Groups wait in the vestibule to see the guests arrive.   The President stands at the head of the staircase to receive them, only descending to the entrance to welcome royalty.   The crowd becomes greater every minute, and overflows the vestibule to the central hall where the sculpture is. Blue ribbons, stars, crosses, and orders become abundant, and relieve with a little colour the sombre black of dinner-dress.   A bishop with a well-turned leg in a silk stocking is an agreeable change from the terrible monotony of trousers. The most picturesque figure to be seen in the gathering of the guests in 1893 was the Cardinal of Westminster, who wore his full canonicals, the first instance of the kind since the foundation of the Academy.   Tall, of commanding presence, made more dignified by his handsome robes, he attracted great interest, and was the observed of all artist-observers, who wished forthwith to sketch or paint his Eminence.

And now a whisper runs through the throng that

the Prince of Wales has arrived. The babel of talk is barely hushed when His Royal Highness may be seen ascending the stairs accompanied by the President. He moves with easy grace among the crowd, shaking hands with a favoured few, exchanging a remark here and there. Presently dinner is announced, and, following Prince and President, the guests go slowly in. Grace is said by the Honorary Chaplain of the Academy, the present Archbishop of York, when all fall to.

As one large dinner has a strong family likeness to every other large dinner, it is unnecessary to describe this. In the course of it, however, there is a little effective incident which may be alluded to. As daylight gradually wanes, the lights are carefully "nursed," so that darkness may not be too visible, until the time for the speeches has come. Then the President proposes the health of the Queen. On the instant the lights flare out to their full brilliancy, all spring to their feet, and the professional singers give with heart and voice the inspiriting strains of the National Anthem.

The dinner over, the company disperse to look at the pictures in the other galleries, or listen to a military band, which discourses most eloquent music till nearly midnight.

All vestiges of the feast are cleared away, the last cab rattles through the quadrangle, diners and waiters have gone homeward, and the Academy, scene of a brilliant evening, is left to darkness and the night-watchman.

At my earlier Academy dinners, in my salad Associate days, I used to be somewhat nervously anxious as to how I should get on with my immediate neighbours. I was apprehensive of admirals and bashful with bishops; but this timidity vanished after one or two experiences. I formed a plan which answered admirably, and gave equal content and satisfaction to my neighbour and myself. It is at once simple and efficacious. By a few judicious remarks or inquiries, I got my neighbour to talk on the all-absorbing topic, self—the topic on which all men will discourse to any length, on which some few are entertaining, and many tedious. You have only to start a man on his tastes or occupations to ensure his continuing as long as you have patience to listen. An interjectional remark of inquiry or assent at intervals acts as a spur to continued talk, and gives you time to leisurely consume your dinner. And you will have the gratification of knowing that by playing the part of a listener well, your neighbour will consider you to be an intelligent fellow, with a fund of common-sense. The vanity of man is surely as great, if not greater, than the vanity of woman. Justice Shallow still lives, and

Falstaff's "Lord, Lord, how subject we old men are to this vice of lying," is as true now as when the words were written—as true as when the world began.

The aged one will often boast of the feats of his youth, and declare that at eighty years of age he is as good as ever; can run, walk, or ride as well now as when five-and-twenty.   I have known some to be as coy about disclosing their actual age as any woman over thirty could be, or like those ladies whose portraits appear in illustrated magazines, and have no age between one-and-twenty and "present day."   Of this sort is the man who can remember no event that happened more than thirty years ago, though we know him to be well on the high-road to seventy.   But enough of frailties and weaknesses.   We have seen the Academy dining in state.   Let us glance at a banquet less ceremonious.

The Royal Academy Club is composed exclusively of members of that body, who dine together six times a year.   The meetings used to be at Willis's Rooms when I first joined, in the chambers of the Dilettanti Society.   Among many portraits of the Fellows were two magnificent Reynoldses, each containing a group.   Of late years the dinners have been held at Limmer's Hotel, Hanover Square. At the first, in January, the ordinary business of the club is transacted, and the place of meeting for the summer outing arranged. No guests are invited to this dinner, but each member is allowed to introduce two to all others. From generation to generation the first Monday in May, the opening day of the Exhibition, has been celebrated at Greenwich, formerly at the "Trafalgar," now at the Ship Hotel. As many of the members use their privilege of inviting two guests, this dinner is the most fully attended of the year. The chairman elected for the evening gives but two toasts, one "the Queen," the other "Honour and glory to the next Exhibition," meaning of course the next Exhibition of the Royal Academy. Before the days of the Great Exhibition of 1851, people did not ask, "Have you been to the Academy?" but "Have you been to the Exhibition?" This toast is said to be coeval with Reynolds, dating from the foundation of the Academy in 1768. The speeches, originally few in number, have increased annually, until the orations threaten to be more numerous, if less lengthy, than those at the Burlington House banquet on the previous Saturday. A strange creature is man! He complains of the boredom of speech-making, yet continues year after year to enunciate the same painful, platitudes and dreary declamations, to which others pretend to listen.

A steamboat is generally chartered for the Greenwich trip, and if there is no rain or east wind to interfere with personal comfort, the trip down is very pleasant, the river with its numberless craft being always picturesque and interesting ; and should the night be clear and bright, the home journey is both enjoyable and impressive, with hundreds of lights reflected in the water, the broad moon dominating all, investing the scene with weird mystery. One more dinner takes place either in June or early in July at some place of interest away from town, such as Knole, Hatfield, Penshurst, &c.

A sub-committee is formed for the purpose of making arrangements for the day, selecting the hotel, dining there, tasting the wines, &c., &c. I was on this committee a year or so ago, with the secretary of the club and another member, making three in all. Windsor had been fixed on as the place of our dinner, and thither the committee went. So little does the artist interest himself in sporting matters, that we were surprised on arriving to find it was one of the days of Ascot races. The space between the Castle and the opposite side of the street was full of life and bustle. Drags, coaches, char-a-bancs, with traps of every description, made the scene lively, and there was much tootling of horns. One of our number, who is a past-master of chaff, which he can administer with the blandest innocence of manner and expression of any man I ever knew, addressed a fellow selling "c'rect cards of the races." "What's up?" says he.—"Why, the races."—"Races? where?"—"Why, at Ascot."—"Indeed; and where is Ascot? is it far from here?" This was the proverbial "last straw." The patience of the card-tout being thoroughly exhausted, he broke out with, "Look here! we don't come out to be made bally laughing-stocks of, if you do," and retreated, looking back every now and then to fire fresh volleys of imprecations and abuse at my friend, till he became lost among the crowd of vehicles. On the day of the dinner the club went up the river on a steam-launch hired for the occasion, lunching on board. At Cookham we landed, looked at poor Walker's grave, and the tablet, the work of H. H. Armstead, erected to his memory in the old church. After a while we re-embarked, came back to Windsor, and dined at the White Hart Hotel, where formerly stood "The Garter Inn," celebrated in the "Merry Wives of Windsor," and thus ended a delightful day.

In June last year we had a pleasant time at the beautiful city of Oxford, visiting Christ Church, Merton Chapel, the noble Bodleian Library, and other places of interest, through which we were most courteously shown by the heads or other officers of the respective colleges. We were further fortunate in having a genial and respected member, Mr. Graham Jackson, to personally conduct us. We passed an hour in the extensive and beautiful garden of Wadham College before dinner ; the meal was served in the hall, which makes a fine old-world dining-room, with panelled walls, hung thickly with portraits by Reynolds, Gainsborough, and by others of lesser note.

The selection of pictures sent in for the Royal Academy Exhibition is as arduous and fatiguing a duty as I ever experienced.   The most casual observer, as the time draws on, must have noticed numbers of covered vans blocking all the approaches leading to Piccadilly ; not that the pictures are taken in there, but at the back of the building, almost at the end of a long passage leading from Burlington Gardens.   This passage is wide enough only for one line of traffic, so the picture-laden van having discharged its pictorial cargo, makes its exit and room for the next.   Towards afternoon on the last sending-in day, the stream overflows not only Burlington Gardens, but some of the quieter streets beyond.   It is like a very large funnel with a very little tube.   By slow degrees the tube is emptied, and by midnight the last van has left its load, and the Academy gates inexorably closed against any unpunctual stragglers.

On the morning of Monday, five weeks before

the opening of the Exhibition, the Council meets for the most important duty of the year. At ten o'clock precisely the President takes the chair in Gallery No. III. in the centre of the row of councilmen, five on each side. On a little round table in front of him is the auctioneer hammer for calling "order," and two mysterious pieces of metal, one shaped like the letter D, the other in form of a X, inserted in long handles. I never saw these used ; they were introduced as a means of learning the votes in case of the President becoming hoarse or losing his voice. To the left of the row, is a larger table, at which the secretary sits and writes in a book the fate of each work when voted. Behind the Council large canvases, chiefly fulllength portraits, are arranged to screen them in some measure from the draught which persistently plays through the galleries, in a way highly conducive to rheumatism. Great-coats, warm caps, railway rugs, and wraps of all kinds keep out some of the cold, but are feeble substitutes for exercise. Some of the hardiest go bareheaded through the ceremony. All being in readiness, the President taps with his hammer, and addresses a few words to the carpenters, telling them on no account to divulge abroad any of the proceedings in the building, when the judging begins. Pictures from the country, sent on the Saturday, are the material first dealt with ; before these are exhausted, the London supply pours in. Expression of opinion is slow at starting, like the bidding for some works of art in an auction-room. As a general rule, the pictures first brought up are of indifferent quality. When watching the stream of incompetent work, I have often thought of the wiseacres of strong arithmetical bias, who by elaborate calculations discover that not more than one minute and some decimal fraction is the average time devoted to the consideration of a picture. But does it require a second of time to form an opinion on the plainness or prettiness of a woman? "You can tell a good picture as you pass in a hackney-coach" is a saying attributed to Constable, and he might have added that the same amount of time would suffice for deciding the badness of several. "Out! out!" is cried in continual chorus, as a stratum of works more than usually bad is discovered. They come in seeming endlessness, and the head-carpenter, keeping his eye on the President, "crosses" their backs at the rate of an Oxford stroke, thirty-five or thirty-six to the minute. Now a hush; the voices eager for rejection a moment ago are soft and low in murmuring admiration for a fine work by some clever outsider. Beauties are pointed out and dwelt on, but time warns that admiration must not be too long indulged in, and the picture is removed to the place of

"accepteds" amid "bravo's," and more rarely clap-
ping of hands.

The next work, though good, suffers from the
brilliancy of its immediate predecessor.   Is it up
to the standard of accept?   We get up and look
closer.   "That's good," says one, pointing out one
portion.   "But that won't do," says another, pointing to another.   The President waits a little.   "Will
you vote on this, gentlemen.   Don't you see a D in
it?"   Hands are held up, five for—five against.
Ever on the side of mercy the President gives the
casting vote, and the picture is carried away to the
rapidly increasing mass of "doubtfuls."

No one is allowed to mention names, or supposed
to be aware of the authorship of any picture.   But
any painter who has seen some half-dozen works
by another can recognise his style, just as any one
knows the handwriting of a friend.   Here is a
picture by a painter which a few know to be the
work of one getting old and infirm, whose hand
begins to lose its cunning, worn by illness, and
anxiety as to the eternal problem of how to
make both ends meet.   The few do all they can,
and stand up for it, but the majority are dead
against it—won't have it; and the unfortunate picture
descends to the cellarage, condemned and rejected.
So the same tune—accept, doubtful, reject—doubtful, reject, accept—continues till one o'clock, when

the welcome sound of the whistle announces the hour of lunch, and Council and carpenters have an hour of rest and restoration. Sharp at two o'clock the judging is resumed and continued till four. Half an hour is allowed for tea, refreshing beverage, which cheers the spirits, brightens the perceptive faculties, and enables one cheerfully to continue the work till six P.M. The selection then is over for the day. A breath even of the smoke-laden atmosphere of Piccadilly is grateful to the eyes and lungs after sitting so many hours, and a brisk walk home gives zest to the evening meal and ensures a good night's rest.

Such is a general outline of the occupation which, with slight variations, lasts from seven to eight days. When the oil-paintings have been looked through, the water-colours and works in black and white, etchings, engravings, drawings, &c., are examined; architecture follows, and sculpture comes last. The Council sits in the water-colour room, to judge the drawings in water-colours and works in black and white, and becomes a more compact group as the works diminish in size. Heads are laid closer together during the inspection of the miniatures, a somewhat tedious process, for each has to be passed from hand to hand. The procession of lugubrious-looking carpenters, each bearing a tiny frame against his chest, as they slowly march to the judgment-seat, seldom fails to excite a smile, as the feeblest joke uttered in a court of justice evokes roars of laughter, and is a welcome relief to the monotony of the proceedings.   All this time the huge lift in the central hall, by the entrance to the lecture-room, is continually and noiselessly at work, ascending with sculpture, or adding acres of painted canvas to the interminable stacks already accumulated.   Anon it descends, laden with un- fortunates that have been found wanting, to the depths below, the cellars of the condemned.   There is something weird and uncanny to me about this lift ; it is associated in fancy with the guillotine. An insatiate and implacable monster, it causes care and despondency to invade many a happy house- hold.   I know of no spectacle more painful and depressing of its kind than is seen in a walk through these cold, whitewashed cellars after the selection is finished.   Stack after stack of pictures, many of them 10, 12, and even 18 feet in length ; their faces turned as if in shame to the wall.   Groups of sculpture, statues, statuettes, busts innumerable, looking grim and ghostly in the gloom, what a mass of frustrated, wasted, human endeavour do they not represent !   Yet blame cannot be imputed to the Royal Academy for this melancholy spectacle. If artists continue to increase and multiply as they have of late years, it is difficult to imagine not only

where they will be enabled to exhibit their works,
but how they will live.   Besides the schools of the
Royal Academy, the Slade, the Herkomer, not to
mention numerous private schools, South Kensington has its enormous and ever-growing army of
art students.   The Science and Art Department
was established in 1857.   In that year the number
of persons receiving art instruction assisted by
State aid was 55,000.   That number has increased
to over 1,270,000!

The hanging of the pictures may be dismissed
in a few words.   The selection finished, the five
members of Council in their second year of office
retire, leaving the arrangement of the Exhibition
to the five who serve in their first year.   Welcome
is the change to active exercise after sitting so
many hours.   The "line" is of course first looked
to, "centres" and the more prominent places decided on, the intervening spaces gradually filled in.
The row above the line follows; pictures, refractory
at first, by coaxing and squeezing find places, and
by slow degrees a "wall" is built up.   In 1869,
the first year that the Academy moved into Burlington House, a space was left between each
picture, much to the benefit of the aspect of the
walls, as well as of the pictures themselves; but
this arrangement became impossible under increased
pressure, and has never been repeated.   When the

topmost row is taken in hand, the "doubtfuls" have a chance; it becomes often a matter of measurement only whether a picture shall obtain a place or be crowded out altogether. Animated discussions are frequent; it is no unusual thing, if the whole or part of a wall be not considered satisfactory, for the works covering it to be taken down and entirely rearranged. As day succeeds day, each is marked by a nearer approach to the end. At length the gigantic puzzle is fitted and put together. A final examination of the whole work is held, as the Council, headed by the President, walks through the galleries. It is decided that all has been done that could be done, and the carpenters are called in to remove the stacks of unfortunate "doubtfuls," for which there is no longer the least hope, to clear away all litter, making everything in order for the morrow, when at ten o'clock the members are admitted to their first varnishing or re-touching day.

Within two months of my election as Associate of the Royal Academy, I had the further honour of being made an Associate of the Royal Society of Painters in Water Colours. I received letters from J. D. Watson and F. Walker the following morning, announcing that I had been unanimously elected, and offering me their congratulations. Watson was a fellow-student with

me at the Royal Academy; we were also proba-
tioners together, and I remember what an admirable pencil-drawing he made of the skeleton. He
was very quiet and reserved in manner, extremely

PORTRAIT OF THE AUTHOR DRAWN BY J. D. WATSON ONE EVENING
AT LANGHAM CHAMBERS.

modest, nay, almost shy, when he came up from
the North, and I first knew him. He took to
drawing on wood, and soon established a reputation
as an illustrator of books and magazines, with the
aid and encouragement of the brothers Dalziel.

Among these, his illustrations to our old friends " Pilgrim's Progress " and " Robinson Crusoe " were very popular. He was a very facile worker as well as versatile, painted both in water-colour and oil, and would certainly have been made a member of the Academy had he only followed up for a few years the success he made with a picture which, though only of a single figure, was dramatically conceived and rendered, called " The Poisoned Cup." It was placed in a centre in the North Room in the year 1866. He was one of the best artists to advise about a picture in progress that I have known. In personal appearance he was tall and handsome. He had one of those faces which seem to improve and become more dignified as time creeps on. In his later days, when his hair, moustache, and pointed beard were of a uniform grey, he looked as if he had stepped out of the frame of one of Vandyke's portraits.

At the close of the year 1883 I was elected full member of the Royal Water Colour Society, and a few weeks afterwards received my diploma signed by the Queen, thus obtaining a second autograph of Her Majesty, who graciously affixes her sign-manual to these documents since she allowed the Society to adopt the title of " Royal." While fully appreciating the honour and favour thus shown to the body, I like still to regard it as the "old" Society, the name by which it is endeared by early associations and Ruskin's writings; the name also which Mr. Roget has adopted as the title of his able and comprehensive work, "The History of the 'Old' Water Colour Society."

There is a homeliness, a simplicity about the abode, the meetings, and the doings of "the little Society," as Walker fondly called it, which are in great contrast with the palatial home and senatorial proceedings of the Royal Academy. But being catholic in taste, I find I can equally enjoy the pleasures and privileges of the palace, and the comfort and quiet of the cottage. The knowledge that I have been deemed worthy by so large a number of my fellow-artists to occupy a position of rank level with their own in two such institutions, has been, and will ever be, one of my proudest and most gratifying reflections.

The duties of members of the Old Water Colour Society are neither numerous nor onerous. The Council meetings, on which they serve in rotation for two succeeding years, are less than a dozen in the twelve months. These, with general and anniversary meetings, cannot be said to make severe inroads on the private working hours of the members. Nor does the arrangement of the annual Spring and Winter Exhibitions absorb an appreciable amount of time. These being confined solely to the works of members and Associates, the long, weary, and depressing duty of selection is avoided. The "hanging" occupies from two to three days at the outside, and from the day on which the works are received at the gallery to that of the private view, less than a fortnight is consumed ; the greater portion of that time being occupied in the preparation and printing of the catalogue. A day is set apart for the contributors to inspect their works, and, if necessary, to touch on them. None are allowed to be taken from the walls till after mid-day, when those who wish to work may have their drawings removed from their frames, and retouch or correct either in the gallery or at their homes, on the understanding that every work must be returned to its place by the evening before the private view.

The gallery now presents a scene of apparently hopeless muddle (common to all exhibitions just before opening), that the inexperienced would suppose it impossible to evoke order out of such confusion. Rough temporary tables are littered with trays of picture rings and screws, colour boxes, wrappers of paper, calico, and waterproof, more paper, rags, and bits of string on the un-swept floors. But all comes right in the end. The carpet is laid down, seats and lounges are divested of their coverings, placed in order, and have their

leathern coats rubbed and brightened. All lumber
is stowed away and hidden, swept and garnished,
spick and span, neat as a new pin, all is ready
for our opening day.

On the fourth Monday in March of each year a
meeting is held for the election of Associates of the
Society. Candidates for the honour are required
to send three finished drawings, framed as for
exhibition, as examples of their work, a week
beforehand. These are hung on the gallery walls,
and on the day of meeting the candidates are
balloted for. They increase in number every year,
and evidence the growing love and study of the
art. The depression from which all commercial
enterprise is suffering arouses the ardour and multi-
plies the numbers of the water-colour artist, as it
does that of his brother who paints in oil. At
the meeting, printed lists of the candidates' names
are distributed to the members, who may mark
or "scratch" as many as he likes. The papers,
gathered together, are placed before the President
who calls out the marked names. Those which
have obtained more than a certain number of
scratches then go to the ballot. Each of these
foremost names has its own ballot-box. I have
seen as many at one meeting as eight or ten,
making a portentous row. As may be easily conceived, the process of voting is somewhat lengthy.

When ended, it will be found not more than two, or at the most three, of the competitors have gained the Associateship.

For some time before an election it is singular what an interest is awakened in many of the competitors as to the health of members. Dormant through the remainder of the year, it becomes lively now. Description, and in some cases little sketches of the drawings by the aspirant, are accompanied by earnest hopes that you are "quite well," and suggestions, more or less broad, that your vote would be most thankfully received. It is scarcely surprising that these tender inquiries about one's physical condition should emanate from the gentler sex.

For upwards of fifty years Sir John Gilbert has been a central figure in British art. Men as diverse in views as Rossetti and Walker, the one a mystic, the other a realist, yet poets both, rendered him homage. More than any artist of our time, he has promoted the interests of illustrated journalism by his genius and example. His marvellous invention and fertility of design, his resources of composition, his brilliant charm of execution, have been at once the despair of students, the wonder of veterans in art. Some time ago Sir John talked of resigning the Presidentship, but a deputation of influential members induced him fortunately to reconsider his determination, and remain our honoured head. A Deputy-President was accordingly appointed to relieve him of the more fatiguing duties of his position or of encountering the risks of night air. Alfred Hunt was the first Deputy-President, 1888–89, Carl Haag the second, 1890–91, and I the last, 1892–93. During my term I served on the Fine Arts Committee of the Chicago Exhibition as representing the Society, but a duty I found more congenial was responding to the toast of " The Royal Water Colour Society" at the dinner of the Artists' General Benevolent Institution at the Hotel Metropolé in May 1892. Some pains were bestowed on this speech, and an endeavour made to import the element of humour, too frequently absent from after-dinner oratory. I am tempted to give it here to enliven the ending of this chapter, more especially as it was marred and mangled in the press reports. Even the *Times*, so admirably accurate as a rule, missed most of the points. After a few phrases of tribute to Sir John, whose unworthy representative I was on the occasion, I spoke as follows :—

" In speaking of water as a vehicle in painting, I claim for it an antiquity so remote that oil, by comparison, can pretend merely to be a modern fad, a thing of yesterday.

" The greasier medium, with all its airs and graces,

may boast a history of a few paltry centuries, and
speak with bated breath of John Van Eyck, but
water-colour long before that time, when in a frail
moment she gave birth to her illegitimate offspring
in oil, could point to a record counted not by
hundreds but by thousands of years. She gave
to Italy her magnificence in fresco, after making

the temple architecture of Egypt glorious in
polychromy.

" But I would go farther than this, and assert that
water-colour is coeval with creation. As our first
parent was created perfect, he must, of necessity,
have been an artist born. It follows that being an
artist, he must have worked in water-colour, for

he was ignorant of glazings, of scumblings, had never heard of megilp or amber varnish, even Roberson's medium was to him unknown. His sketches from nature, which must have included the nude, were unquestionably dashed off in water-colour. Thus, while the Royal Academy claims Sir Joshua Reynolds as its founder, we of the Royal Water Colour Society are as artists proud of our descent from the father of mankind.

"Though water-colour is not ashamed of her oleaginous offspring, yet, by the claims of superior age, and the homage due to her, she admonishes oil to hide her diminished head, and, in the polished vernacular of the day, to take a back seat."

END OF VOL. I.

Printed by BALLANTYNE, HANSON & Co.
Edinburgh and London

www.ingramcontent.com/pod-product-compliance
Lightning Source LLC
Chambersburg PA
CBHW031406270326
41929CB00010BA/1354